LETS
GO
PUBLISH
!

Dedication

Each & Every day when I would go to work in the front office, and sometimes even before I would arrive, my two co-workers on every book project were there to greet me and work with me all day—other than for extremely necessary bio-breaks for all parties.

This book is dedicated to these two fine individuals Benny, the first little man, passed away a month ago but his spirit is with me.
Buddy does his best to make up for Ben's absence.

Ben & Dad

Buddy, Ben & Mom

Acknowledgments:

I appreciate all the help that I have received in putting this book together as well as all the other 98 books from the past.

My acknowledgments were so large at one time that readers complained that they had to go through too many pages to get to page one.

And, so I put my acknowledgment list online, and it continues to grow. Believe it or not, it costs about a dollar less to print my books today than then. No kidding!

Thank you my dear friends and supporters of many years. May God bless you all for your help.

You may check out www.letsgopublish.com to read the latest version of my heartfelt acknowledgments updated for this book.

Thank you all very much!

Brian

Preface:

Many people were introduced to Donald Trump for the first time when they heard him say: "We're going to build a wall and Mexico is going to pay for it." President Trump often spoke about the wall but he also spoke about many other notions for our country that will help make America great again!

President Trump lived through the last eight years like the rest of us and he knows that our country lost a lot of zip during the Obama years. President Donald J. Trump is the perfect president to bring our nation back bigger and better than ever before.

Since the first time we heard it, the President has fine-tuned his wall message into a textual work of art: "I will build a great wall -- and nobody builds walls better than me, believe me --and I'll build them very inexpensively. I will build a great, great wall on our southern border, and I will make Mexico pay for that wall. Mark my words."

We get your message, Mr. President, and we believe you and we believe in you. Thank you!

Our new President also made a number of other campaign promises on the trail. These are aimed at changes to immigration, trade, taxes and foreign policy. He has also rejected and repudiated the narratives of the elites, and besides bringing jobs back as a president elect, his election on November 8 is also responsible for having the country say "Merry Christmas" again. President Trump likes saying Merry Christmas for sure and the people I know feel that in many ways, Donald J. Trump as President was their best Christmas present ever.

Let's list ten of President Trump's campaign promises as these will be part of the building blocks for our new President to make America great again:

1. Build the wall and make Mexico pay for it
2. Temporarily ban Muslims from entering the United States
3. Bring US manufacturing (jobs) back from overseas
4. Impose tariffs on goods made in China and Mexico
5. Renegotiate or withdraw from the NAFTA and TPP trade agreements
6. Full repeal of Obamacare' and replace it with a market-based (not government) alternative
7. Renegotiate the Iran deal
8. Keep Social Security intact & Increase Benefits
9. Cut taxes
10. Wipe ISIS from the face of the Earth and take their oil

Some have characterized these as vague promises but they look solid to me. Others suggest that the President's appeal is not necessarily from these promises about what he'll do but from how he talks about them. Larry Sabato, for example, of UVA says "As long as non-college, blue-collar whites like the sound of these promises, Trump will keep repeating them."

I have never seen the country as positively charged as I do now. I was away with some friends over the Inauguration weekend, and out of eighteen of us, there was just one staunch Hillary supporter. We tried to be kind and were. We were reminded of his past actions and were told outright that if the shoe were on the other foot, he'd be hammering us all.

During this weekend, seventeen people of like mind were all acting out like as if it were still Christmas in the US and. Even a crass and dirty Madonna could not dampen our spirits.

So, don't let the corrupt press fool you. There are tons of us out here. We have to prick ourselves with pins every now and then to prove that we are still real and not in a big Toon Town happy dream. It is great to wake up to find Donald J. Trump as President of the US.

In addition to the precepts outlined above as Trump promises, there are several other great ideas that President Trump may adopt to make his presidency much more special than any that have ever come before him.

Even without these additional suggestions for adoption, I admit that I see the Trump Presidency grabbing a place in history that might be characterized in the same great adjectives that we use to describe our founding. After suffering through an eight-year period in which many of us believed the President was indifferent at best towards Americans and who did not like much about America, it is refreshing to have real hope for great things to come. Whereas Obama seemed hell bent on giving us a comeuppance, Donald Trump wants to make America great again. Big difference.

I had the pleasure during the campaign of selling a number of 2016 books that I wrote to help Candidate Trump win the election. I gave many of the books away at events such as Chris Cox's Biker rallies. They were well received. I loved helping. This is the people's victory

President Trump has the best of the best advising him right now and I do not want to appear presumptuous by introducing competing notions to those on the list above. The list of additional ideas and how-to' s for the President, however, are not on his list per se and they offer a people's perspective about areas that he perhaps he has not considered. I think they can help his overall platform and present them in that light.

Each of these is a book title and each of the books explains in detail how to achieve benefits from the notions described within the books. Just like this book, which you are reading, the based-on books are also available on Amazon and Kindle. The Trump Way was a series I put together in the summer 2016. I am in the process of writing a new series which will be an update to each of the books in the Trump Way and perhaps a few more. The New series is known as The Master Builder Series.

Here is the list for Mr. Trump to consider as part of making America great again:

1. Why Trump?
2. President Donald J. Trump Master Builder: The Annual Guest Plan
3. Saving America—The Trump Way   23
4. Reduce, Repeal, Reindustrialize, Raise, Revitalize, Remember (RRRRRR)—The Trump Way
5. Jobs! Jobs! Jobs!—The Trump Way   53
6. 101 Secrets How To Be A High Information Voter
7. Healthcare & Welfare Accountability—The Trump Way
8. Take the Train to Myrtle Beach—The Trump Way
9. The Trump Plan Solves the Student Debt Crisis
10. Seniors, Social Security, & the Minimum Wage—a Trump Perspective

My first recommendation is for the Trump Administration to implement the crowning jewel of all of my recommendations to President Trump. It is reflected in the first book that I have written since the election. It is also the first book written in the Master Builder series. It's title is:

President Donald J. Trump Master Builder: The Annual Guest Plan

Before I close out this preface, please permit me to give a perspective on the Annual Guest Plan (AGP). The AGP is a unique plan that places the needs of America and Americans first. It solves the problem of 20 to 60 million illegal interlopers in residence in the US.

The Annual Guest Plan is intended to be the secret sauce of President Trump's US Immigration Fix. Yes—build the wall, please! But simultaneously solve the residence problem. Do we really need up to 60 million interlopers in residence?

This book is the result of over ten years of work from way back when I wrote my first patriotic book in 2006 titled *Taxation without Representation.*

Ideally, the solution would be to go *poof,* and every foreign interloper would be taken back to where and when they crossed the border—years and years ago. Where are the used Star-Trek Transporters when we need one?

This time, however, the interlopers would be turned back if they tried to cross, and the problem would not ever have gotten to the level of severity that it is today. Even though Mr. Trump has already done some magic, even he makes no claim of having the ability to perform miracles.

A key element of the plan is that each year the clock resets on foreign nationals who are permitted here under the Annual Guest Plan. This book, thus focuses on interlopers registering and then signing up for $100 per year to become Annual Guests with appropriate renewal assurances for good behavior. They get zero benefits and cost zero to taxpayers; cannot be citizens; cannot vote; and cannot get a job ahead of an American. There are many other aspects of this plan that make it nothing like amnesty. You'll like it and if I can ever get it before President Trump, he'll like it too.

I wrote this book to help Americans know what our President and Congress can do to force our government to regain control of our borders, ensure our national security, keep our culture, enforce our laws, protect American jobs, make our language the language of the nation, and keep all Americans from being overwhelmed by illegal foreign nationals who take from the taxpayers, offer few benefits and have no allegiance to America.

End of information on *Donald J. Trump Master Builder: The Annual Guest Plan*

Thank you for indulging me this small commercial about a topic which takes up a full chapter in this book "Make America Great

Again", as well as being the lead book in the Master Builder Series.

You are going to love this book, the kickoff book to the Master Builder Series. Few books are a must-read but President Donald J Trump, Master Builder: "Make America Great Again." will quickly appear at the top of America's most read list. Please ask President Trump to check out all of the books in this new series and adopt all of the America-First principles that he deems appropriate.

Thank You All Very Much

Table of Contents

About the Author

Brian W. Kelly retired as an Assistant Professor in the Business Information Technology (BIT) program at Marywood University, where he also served as the IBM i and midrange systems technical advisor to the IT Faculty. Kelly has designed, developed, and taught many college and professional courses. He is also a contributing technical editor to a number of IT industry magazines, including "The Four Hundred" and "Four Hundred Guru" published by IT Jungle.

Kelly is a former IBM Senior Systems Engineer and he was a candidate for US Congress from Pennsylvania. He has an active information technology consultancy. He is the author of 100 books, in many topical areas, as well as hundreds of articles. This is Brian's 100th published book. Kelly has been a frequent speaker at many US conferences.

When Kelly ran for Congress as a Democrat against a 13-term Democrat in 2010, he took no campaign contributions, spent just enough to buy signs and T-shirts, and as a virtual unknown, he captured 17% of the vote. Kelly says: "Writing books is lots easier than running for public office!"

Chapter 1 President Donald J. Trump, Master Builder: Against All Odds!

All the wagers were bets against Trump

Despite the odds, polls, and projections, Donald Trump emerged as the big victor in the presidential election late on Tuesday evening November 8, 2016 and into Wednesday morning. Trump delivered a fine speech at the Hilton Hotel in New York City to a cheering crowd of supporters. "Make America Great Again!"

Nobody seemed to think he would win except for his following of John Does across the country. To say it was an unexpected outcome for the Republican candidate is a major understatement. Mr. Trump not only beat out one of the best GOP primary fields of all-time, but he also beat a well-seasoned and perhaps even more formidable opponent in Hillary Clinton.

Mrs. Clinton seemed almost complacent near the end of the campaign giving off signs that she knew she had won. She was consistently ahead of Candidate Trump in the polls up and she seemed to be in an even stronger position on the electoral map. Few odds makers around the world favored Donald Trump. Yet, regular Joes who came out in the tens of thousands every campaign stop somehow knew the polls were wrong. Regular people from the heartland of America and the rustbelt put Mr. Trump over the top.

Candidate Trump never got a break during the campaign from a corrupt, biased media who often cleared their talking points with

Mrs. Clinton before going on the air. Sometimes they even gave the Clinton camp the answers in debates.

Despite all odds, Trump definitely struck a chord with the American people as an unorthodox candidate without any political background—other than the politics of winning and the politics of making deals and taking the prize.

Trump called for a Southern border wall, a temporary ban on Muslim immigrants, and he had major opposition to our poorly negotiated trade deals. The press called these notions "bombastic," but they played well with Americans looking to have somebody in charge willing to "drain the swamp" and of course to make America great again!

In the final debate with Mrs. Clinton, there was a bruhaha about Trump's possible refusal to concede the election. Ironically, though Mrs Clinton ultimately conceded, she sponsored a number of actions meant to disrupt the peaceful transition of power such as numerous recounts and of course blaming her loss on the Russians. It was all viewed as whiny and silly by most regular Americans.

President-Elect Trump's Acceptance Speech on Election Day

Thank you. Thank you very much, everyone. Sorry to keep you waiting. Complicated business, complicated. Thank you very much.

I've just received a call from Secretary Clinton. She congratulated us. It's about us. On our victory, and I congratulated her and her family on a very, very hard-fought campaign.

I mean, she fought very hard. Hillary has worked very long and very hard over a long period of time, and we owe her a major debt of gratitude for her service to our country.

It is time. I pledge to every citizen of our land that I will be president for all of Americans, and this is so important to me. For those who have chosen not to support me in the past, of which there were a few people, I'm reaching out to you for your guidance and your help so that we can work together and unify our great country. As I've said from the beginning, ours was not a campaign but rather an incredible and great movement, made up of millions of hard-working men and women who love their country and want a better, brighter future for themselves and for their family.

It is a movement comprised of Americans from all races, religions, backgrounds, and beliefs, who want and expect our government to serve the people, and serve the people it will.

Working together, we will begin the urgent task of rebuilding our nation and renewing the American dream. I've spent my entire life in business, looking at the untapped potential in projects and in people all over the world.

That is now what I want to do for our country. Tremendous potential. I've gotten to know our country so well. Tremendous potential. It is going to be a beautiful thing. Every single American will have the opportunity to realize his or her fullest potential. The forgotten men and women of our country will be forgotten no longer.

We are going to fix our inner cities and rebuild our highways, bridges, tunnels, airports, schools, hospitals. We're going to rebuild our infrastructure, which will become, by the way, second to none, and we will put millions of our people to work as we rebuild it. We will also finally take care of our great veterans who have been so loyal, and I've gotten to know so many over this 18-month journey.

The time I've spent with them during this campaign has been among my greatest honors.

Our veterans are incredible people. We will embark upon a project of national growth and renewal. I will harness the creative talents of our people, and we will call upon the best and brightest to leverage their tremendous talent for the benefit of all. It is going to happen. We have a great economic plan. We will double our growth and have the strongest economy anywhere in the world. At the same time, we will get along with all other nations willing to get along with us. We will be. We will have great relationships. We expect to have great, great relationships. No dream is too big, no challenge is too great. Nothing we want for our future is beyond our reach.

America will no longer settle for anything less than the best. We must reclaim our country's destiny and dream big and bold and daring. We have to do that. We're going to dream of things for our country, and beautiful things and successful things once again.

I want to tell the world community that while we will always put America's interests first, we will deal fairly with everyone, with everyone.

All people and all other nations. We will seek common ground, not hostility; partnership, not conflict. And now I would like to take this moment to thank some of the people who really helped me with this, what they are calling tonight a very, very historic victory.

First, I want to thank my parents, who I know are looking down on me right now. Great people. I've learned so much from them. They were wonderful in every regard. Truly great parents. I also want to thank my sisters, Marianne and Elizabeth, who are here with us tonight. Where are they? They're here someplace. They're very shy, actually.

And my brother Robert, my great friend. Where is Robert? Where is Robert?

My brother Robert, and they should be on this stage, but that's okay. They're great.

And also my late brother Fred, great guy. Fantastic guy. Fantastic family. I was very lucky.

Great brothers, sisters, great, unbelievable parents. To Melania and Don and Ivanka and Eric and Tiffany and Barron, I love you and I thank you, and especially for putting up with all of those hours. This was tough.

This was tough. This political stuff is nasty, and it is tough. So I want to thank my family very much. Really fantastic. Thank you all. Thank you all. Lara, unbelievable job. Unbelievable. Vanessa, thank you. Thank you very much. What a great group.

You've all given me such incredible support, and I will tell you that we have a large group of people. You know, they kept saying we have a small staff. Not so small. Look at all of the people that we have. Look at all of these people.

And Kellyanne and Chris and Rudy and Steve and David. We have got tremendously talented people up here, and I want to tell you it's been very, very special.

I want to give a very special thanks to our former mayor, Rudy Giuliani. He's unbelievable. Unbelievable. He traveled with us and he went through meetings, and Rudy never changes. Where is Rudy. Where is he?

[Chanting "Rudy"]

Gov. Chris Christie, folks, was unbelievable. Thank you, Chris. The first man, first senator, first major, major politician — let me tell you, he is highly respected in Washington because he is as smart as you get. Sen. Jeff Sessions. Where is Jeff? A great man. Another great man, very tough competitor. He was not easy. He was not easy. Who is that? Is that the mayor that showed up? Is that Rudy?

Up here. Really a friend to me, but I'll tell you, I got to know him as a competitor because he was one of the folks that was negotiating to go against those Democrats, Dr. Ben Carson. Where's been? Where is Ben? By the way, Mike Huckabee is here someplace, and he is fantastic. Mike and his familiar bring Sarah, thank you very much. Gen. Mike Flynn. Where is Mike? And Gen. Kellogg. We have over 200 generals and admirals that have endorsed our campaign and there are special people.

We have 22 Congressional Medal of Honor people. A very special person who, believe me, I read reports that I wasn't getting along with him. I never had a bad second with him. He's an unbelievable star. He is — that's right, how did you possibly guess? Let me tell you about Reince. I've said Reince. I know it. I know it. Look at all of those people over there. I know it, Reince is a superstar. I said, they can't call you a superstar, Reince, unless we win it. Like Secretariat. He would not have that bust at the track at Belmont.

Reince is really a star and he is the hardest-working guy, and in a certain way I did this. Reince, come up here. Get over here, Reince.

Boy, oh, boy, oh, boy. It's about time you did this right. My god. Nah, come here. Say something.

[Reince Priebus: Ladies and gentlemen, the next president of the united States, Donald Trump! Thank you. It's been an honor. God bless. Thank God.]

Amazing guy. Our partnership with the RNC was so important to the success and what we've done, so I also have to say, I've gotten to know some incredible people.

The Secret Service people. They're tough and they're smart and they're sharp and I don't want to mess around with them, I can tell ya. And when I want to go and wave to a big group of people and they rip me down and put me back down in the seat, but they are fantastic people so I want to thank the Secret Service.

And law enforcement in New York City, they're here tonight. These are spectacular people, sometimes underappreciated unfortunately. We appreciate them. So, it's been what they call an historic event, but to be really historic, we have to do a great job, and I promise you that I will not let you down. We will do a great job. We will do a great job. I look very much forward to being your president, and hopefully at the end of two years or three years or four years or maybe even eight years you will say so many of you worked so hard for us, with you. You will say that — you will say that that was something that you were — really were very proud to do and I can — thank you very much.

And I can only say that while the campaign is over, our work on this movement is now really just beginning. We're going to get to work immediately for the American people, and we're going to be doing a job that hopefully you will be so proud of your president. You will be so proud. Again, it's my honor.

It's an amazing evening. It's been an amazing two-year period, and I love this country. Thank you.

Thank you very much. Thank you to Mike Pence.

--end of Trump Acceptance Speech ---

After the fanfare, the press kept at the President elect finding one fault after another. It seemed every day, they dug up another untruth meant to delegitimatize the new President-Elect. This emboldened Trump supporters who fully understood the corruption in the media.

President Donald Trump took office with a modest degree of fanfare on January 20, 2017 with a big promise to "Make America Great Again."

He came a long way over 18 months from when he first announced his candidacy on June 16, 2015. You may recall the words with which he kicked off his campaign: "So, ladies and gentlemen, I am officially running for president of the United States, and we are going to make our country great again." Now as I write this first paragraph one day before the Trump Inauguration, we all know one thing for sure: "He was not kidding." Quite frankly, I am thrilled as are about one out of ten people that I know.

What a difference time makes. When he announced, the new President was mocked by the press and both political parties, while folks like me welcomed him to the foray. He did not think like the corrupt elite establishment politicians and that was enough for many of us who wanted them all gone.

Somehow these thieves and scoundrels who had cooperated with Obama in the demise of the country for eight years, thought Trump was not worthy of their cozy rich-guy donor clubs. For example, the Trump candidacy sparked ire and intrigue for groups such as the Club for Growth, which foolishly pushed for Trump being banned from the Republican presidential debates. What a bunch of doofuses.

For the record, The Club for Growth is chartered as a 501-type conservative organization active in the United States. Their agenda is supposedly focused on cutting taxes and other economic issues but regular folks like you and I may see them as a bunch of self-centered, grabby, pompous, me-first elite establishment types that do not have a minute for the John Does out in the regular life areas of the country where we live.

The Club for Growth's nasty press release after Mr. Trump's announcement shows what a slime-ball group it is:

"Donald Trump is a great entertainer and developer, but his ideas of what to do as president won't grow the economy," said Club for Growth President David McIntosh.

"The Club for Growth has issued very substantive and detailed white papers on the records of the major announced Republican candidates for president. There is no need to do a white paper on Donald Trump. He is not a serious Republican candidate, and many of his positions make him better suited to take on Hillary Clinton in the Democratic primary. It would also be unfortunate if he takes away a spot at even one Republican debate. The 2016 Republican presidential field is already the most pro-growth in recent history, with great ideas for cutting taxes, repealing Obamacare and replacing it with patient-centered, free market reforms, and moving the country forward with free trade."

David McIntosh, as you can see from his own nasty words, is little more than a pompous ass, who doesn't deserve the opportunity to shine President Donald Trump's shoes or lick his boots.

Guess what Mr. McIntosh, you were and continue to be as wrong as anybody on earth has ever been wrong. Donald Trump is now our new President. You were not smart enough to see that coming yet a bunch of us regular guys who suffered through a do-nothing Republican-led Congress for eight years spawned on by the fat-cat donor class such as your club, could not be more pleased that you are very wrong. Donald Trump is a few weeks into Making America Great Again, and the country can feel a major sense of positivism in the air.

The Club for Growth did put its money where McIntosh's mouth was as it wagered a whopping $7 million in an all-on assault on Trump. They continued their rhetoric that Mr. Trump was nothing more than a Manhattan business mogul and reality TV star and was not even close to being a fiscal or social conservative. The Club for Growth proved that all the money in the world does not make up for good old fashioned smarts. Stupid is as stupid does.

It sure seems that the US could do well without fat-cat pro-amnesty groups such as Club for Growth. When you pick on President Trump, you can always expect a return volley. Before and after the election, President Trump repeatedly accused Club for Growth of airing attack ads against him because he refused to give the conservative group a $1 million donation – or what Trump calls "a form of extortion." Keep your money fat cats; our guy is now the President.

Mr. Trump had lots of problems with weepy and wimpy sore loser Republicans such as the all of the Bush's, Lynsdey Graham, John McCain, Glenn Beck and others too proud to check their whining at the door. Yet, he prevailed and he is now the President. Life is already getting better.

Unlike how he was characterized as a man without a plan, President Donald J. Trump has many detailed plans for how to attack his mission. He has explained in detail the bills and reforms he says will revitalize the American economy, generate jobs, and strengthen and restore America's standing on the international stage. Donald Trump is taking action every day to make America great again!

Here are several precepts President Trump has been talking about for quite a while. Just like he got several companies to change their job plans before he took the oath, he is remaining active and is moving forward on his plans:

President Donald Trump does not like the idea of America being pushed around militarily or economically. US partners will be doing a lot of cost-sharing, which will reduce U.S. costs and guarantee that veterans and their families are protected. My money is and has been on Trump, "Money is itself a weapon," says President Trump.

For example, from day one he has suggested that America should not be spending trillions of dollars fighting other nations' battles and they "get the oil." Trump says:

"Why are we footing the bill and getting nothing in return?...

"I'll give you the answer. It's because our so-called 'leaders' in Washington know absolutely nothing about negotiations and deal making."

President Trump is not a friend of OPEC. He uses the term NOPEC to describe what he would like to see as our new "OPEC" relationship.

He wants NOPEC legislation on the table so we can break this anti-American conglomerate's grip on US energy prices. Trump says, "It is time to get tough." Who does not agree?

"Imagine how much money the average American would save if we busted the OPEC cartel. Imagine how much stronger economic shape we would be in if we made the Iraqi government agree to a cost-sharing plan that paid us back the $1.5 trillion we've dropped on liberating Iraq."

President Trump knows how to find big deals to help America: "Just those two acts of leadership alone would represent a huge leap forward for our country."

China and Currency

Throughout the campaign, in debates and in speeches, President Trump continually called for a major crackdown on the currency manipulation, which has become part of China's MO. Mr. Trump said we should tax their imports based upon the true dollar of the currency – based on how much a manufacturing company's currency has been devalued.

Though President Trump believes in free trade, he thinks that the US has time and again sent the fourth team or worse to negotiate our trade deals. He says we are always out-played. The US should not have to compete when the rules are unfair and currency is not properly valued. In his speeches, he cites a study by the Peterson Institute for International Economics that found that that even a 20 percent revaluation of Chinese currency would create 300,000 to 700,000 American jobs.

"Getting China to stop playing its currency charades can begin whenever we elect a president ready to take decisive action .... It would allow our government to calculate taxes on imports based on how much the manufacturing country's currency is undervalued."

"It's the utter weakness and failure to fight for American interests from Geithner and Obama that have left us underwriting China's economic rise and our own economic collapse," writes Trump. "It's a plain fact: free trade requires having fair rules that apply to everyone."

Job and Wealth Creation

President Trump remembers how President Obama called all the CEOS of the car manufacturers to Washington and they all came in private planes. CEOs including President Obama and Air Force One—before January 21, optimize their time by having their own transportation. President Obama tried to make them all look like jerks because they did not fly commercial. Donald Trump is no dummy and he knows that most CEOs are not dummies.

"People are smart," writes Trump. "They know you can't be 'for' jobs and against those who create them." Obama, who is a documented business hater, never quite got that

Trump has a tax plan to spur job and wealth creation. Trump's plan has five parts intended to spark economic growth and allow Americans to keep more of what they earn. Here are the five parts:

1. The U.S. must repeal the death tax.
2. Lowering tax rate on capital gains and dividends.
3. Reduce the corporate tax rate to zero. Recently President Trump has advocated bringing it to about 10%. I like zero better. Trump wants foreign companies to relocate their businesses to the United States and create jobs here."
4. The plan also includes a fairer and simpler income tax from 1 % to 15%
5. Finish the Border Fence, Boot Out Criminal Illegals, and Reform America's Legal Immigration System "The GAO says that the annual price tag to incarcerate [illegal alien] thugs is $1.1 billion. And get this: criminal aliens have an average of seven arrests." Mr. Trump says criminal illegal aliens must go and that the Commander-in-Chief must enforce existing immigration laws and finish the border

fence… "properly built walls work. We just need the political will to finish the job."

Trump's book Time to get Tough is a good read. It lays out several more detailed conservative policy reforms, including cracking down on entitlement fraud, ending Obamacare, and reforming America's ever-growing welfare state. As President Trump puts it. *"America needs a safety net, not a hammock."*

The GOP establishment has been eager right from the get-go to dismiss Trump's candidacy. Donald J. Trump is now the President and he is in the driver's seat. Like it or not, President Trump has serious policy plans to offer—and he certainly has the star power and the savvy to make them heard and he has the touch of the Master Builder to get them all implemented… not just one—all!

Now, let's move forward into the next chapters in which we get to present ideas to the President. Many of these ideas have previously been written in books authored by yours truly. For example, I wrote ten books in the summer of 2016, the objective of which was to get Donald Trump elected as president. I have seen smatterings of my content in some of Mr. Trump's espoused precepts to help make America great again. I am honored. He can have them all as long as the most comes of these ideas. I am American first and an author second.

Before we look at some new ideas, let's take a nice relaxing look at the President's Inaugural Address. Enjoy!

Chapter 2 President Trump's 2017 Inauguration Address

Great Speech by 45th President of the United States

Like many tuned-in Americans, on January 20, I had the opportunity to observe our 45th president be sworn into office. It has become a tradition to watch the inauguration every four years. Yes, I watched Obama's two inaugurations. I did not enjoy them but I watched them anyway. I really enjoyed President Donald J. Trump taking the oath of office today because I know exactly what it means. Mr. Trump is President of the United States for the next four years and more than likely, the next eight years.

Unlike Trump haters who I knew would find something dark in his speech, for those of us looking for a new guy with a new way of doing things, the speech was the perfect reassurance. Though I still am a conservative, I have learned that I am also a Nationalist and a Populist. Years ago, I bought two web sites—AmericaforAmericans.com and OrdinaryCitizens.com.

I have said America and Americans First many times. It is how I think and I am not Hitlerian, a new word from the left/s Chris Matthews. It just felt so good to hear President Trump say it. Didn't it? I had never tuned into it being a nationalist notion. I love America. We all have reason to be very happy; but we must watch that we are not too smug. Let's permit our liberal friends to come to like President Trump without you and I spoiling it for them as much as we may like to do so.

For now, I thought you would like to read Mr. Trump's great Inauguration Speech. To me it is very uplifting. This is our new President saying things we have hoped to hear for eight years and probably eight before that. Here goes:

Below is the full text of President Trump's inaugural speech:

Chief Justice Roberts, President Carter, President Clinton, President Bush, President Obama, fellow Americans, and people of the world: thank you.

We, the citizens of America, are now joined in a great national effort to rebuild our country and to restore its promise for all of our people.

Together, we will determine the course of America and the world for years to come.

We will face challenges. We will confront hardships. But we will get the job done.

Every four years, we gather on these steps to carry out the orderly and peaceful transfer of power, and we are grateful to President Obama and First Lady Michelle Obama for their gracious aid throughout this transition. They have been magnificent.

Today's ceremony, however, has very special meaning. Because today we are not merely transferring power from one Administration to another, or from one party to another – but we are transferring power from Washington, D.C. and giving it back to you, the American People.

For too long, a small group in our nation's Capital has reaped the rewards of government while the people have borne the cost.

Washington flourished – but the people did not share in its wealth.

Politicians prospered – but the jobs left, and the factories closed.

The establishment protected itself, but not the citizens of our country.

Their victories have not been your victories; their triumphs have not been your triumphs; and while they celebrated in our nation's Capital, there was little to celebrate for struggling families all across our land.

That all changes – starting right here, and right now, because this moment is your moment: it belongs to you.

It belongs to everyone gathered here today and everyone watching all across America.

This is your day. This is your celebration.

And this, the United States of America, is your country.

What truly matters is not which party controls our government, but whether our government is controlled by the people.

January 20th 2017, will be remembered as the day the people became the rulers of this nation again.

The forgotten men and women of our country will be forgotten no longer.

Everyone is listening to you now.

You came by the tens of millions to become part of a historic movement the likes of which the world has never seen before.

At the center of this movement is a crucial conviction: that a nation exists to serve its citizens.

Americans want great schools for their children, safe neighborhoods for their families, and good jobs for themselves.

These are the just and reasonable demands of a righteous public.

But for too many of our citizens, a different reality exists: Mothers and children trapped in poverty in our inner cities; rusted-out factories scattered like tombstones across the landscape of our nation; an education system, flush with cash, but which leaves our young and beautiful students deprived of knowledge; and the crime and gangs and drugs that have stolen too many lives and robbed our country of so much unrealized potential.

This American carnage stops right here and stops right now.

We are one nation – and their pain is our pain. Their dreams are our dreams; and their success will be our success. We share one heart, one home, and one glorious destiny.

The oath of office I take today is an oath of allegiance to all Americans.

For many decades, we've enriched foreign industry at the expense of American industry;

Subsidized the armies of other countries while allowing for the very sad depletion of our military;

We've defended other nation's borders while refusing to defend our own;

And spent trillions of dollars overseas while America's infrastructure has fallen into disrepair and decay.

We've made other countries rich while the wealth, strength, and confidence of our country has disappeared over the horizon.

One by one, the factories shuttered and left our shores, with not even a thought about the millions upon millions of American workers left behind.

The wealth of our middle class has been ripped from their homes and then redistributed across the entire world.

But that is the past. And now we are looking only to the future.

We assembled here today are issuing a new decree to be heard in every city, in every foreign capital, and in every hall of power.

From this day forward, a new vision will govern our land.

From this moment on, it's going to be America First.

Every decision on trade, on taxes, on immigration, on foreign affairs, will be made to benefit American workers and American families.

We must protect our borders from the ravages of other countries making our products, stealing our companies, and destroying our jobs. Protection will lead to great prosperity and strength.

I will fight for you with every breath in my body – and I will never, ever let you down.

America will start winning again, winning like never before.

We will bring back our jobs. We will bring back our borders. We will bring back our wealth. And we will bring back our dreams.

We will build new roads, and highways, and bridges, and airports, and tunnels, and railways all across our wonderful nation.

We will get our people off of welfare and back to work – rebuilding our country with American hands and American labor.

We will follow two simple rules: Buy American and Hire American.

We will seek friendship and goodwill with the nations of the world – but we do so with the understanding that it is the right of all nations to put their own interests first.

We do not seek to impose our way of life on anyone, but rather to let it shine as an example for everyone to follow.

We will reinforce old alliances and form new ones – and unite the civilized world against Radical Islamic Terrorism, which we will eradicate completely from the face of the Earth.

At the bedrock of our politics will be a total allegiance to the United States of America, and through our loyalty to our country, we will rediscover our loyalty to each other.

When you open your heart to patriotism, there is no room for prejudice.

The Bible tells us, "how good and pleasant it is when God's people live together in unity."

We must speak our minds openly, debate our disagreements honestly, but always pursue solidarity.

When America is united, America is totally unstoppable.

There should be no fear – we are protected, and we will always be protected.

We will be protected by the great men and women of our military and law enforcement and, most importantly, we are protected by God.

Finally, we must think big and dream even bigger.

In America, we understand that a nation is only living as long as it is striving.

We will no longer accept politicians who are all talk and no action – constantly complaining but never doing anything about it.

The time for empty talk is over. Now arrives the hour of action. Do not let anyone tell you it cannot be done. No challenge can match the heart and fight and spirit of America.

We will not fail. Our country will thrive and prosper again.

We stand at the birth of a new millennium, ready to unlock the mysteries of space, to free the Earth from the miseries of disease, and to harness the energies, industries and technologies of tomorrow.

A new national pride will stir our souls, lift our sights, and heal our divisions.

It is time to remember that old wisdom our soldiers will never forget: that whether we are black or brown or white, we all bleed the same red blood of patriots, we all enjoy the same glorious freedoms, and we all salute the same great American Flag.

And whether a child is born in the urban sprawl of Detroit or the windswept plains of Nebraska, they look up at the same night sky, they fill their heart with the same dreams, and they are infused with the breath of life by the same almighty Creator.

So to all Americans, in every city near and far, small and large, from mountain to mountain, and from ocean to ocean, hear these words:

You will never be ignored again.

Your voice, your hopes, and your dreams, will define our American destiny. And your courage and goodness and love will forever guide us along the way.

Together, We Will Make America Strong Again.

We Will Make America Wealthy Again.

We Will Make America Proud Again.

We Will Make America Safe Again.

And, Yes, Together, We Will Make America Great Again.

Thank you, God Bless You, And God Bless America.

Chapter 3 Why Trump?

Why Trump, really?

In a book about "Make America Great Again," we get to learn more about why President Trump is determined to accomplish his self-defined mission. The facts are what inspired my first original Donald Trump book this past summer. It is titled, "Why Trump?" and it is still available on Amazon & Kindle.

I knew the answer to "Why Trump," when I wrote the book and published it on August 4, 2016, but I figured this book needed to provide the answer for everybody else. And, so, the book does just that for readers of the paperback and the kindle versions. It answers the simple question: "Why Trump?" *Why Trump* in many ways describes why and how President Donald Trump plans to "Make America Great Again!"

At the time, I was well on-board the Trump Train, hoping the book would bring Mr. Trump and company into Union Station in Washington DC on January 20 right on time. I am pleased to say, the train has arrived and just several minutes ago, I saw President Trump leave the Blair House with his family for the trek over to St. John's Episcopal Church, the Church of Presidents.

Here are some of the salient parts of the "*Why Trump*" book as they can help us all be confident that Mr. Trump, now as President will definitely "Make America Great Again!" Amen! This is the book's introduction from Amazon:

"Why Trump" Introduction

Donald Trump is the only candidate for president who offers Americans a breath of fresh air from the stodgy, bossy, establishment elites in both the Democratic and Republican Party. Trump is against the status quo of rich donors controlling the government for their personal benefit.

Donald J. Trump is a Nationalist [and Populist] with great values. Look at the goodness he instilled into his own children. He is not a liberal fool or a progressive socialist who hates America. He is simply for America and Americans First.

The corrupt mainstream press controlled by the Democratic Party won't give Donald Trump an inch. If Mr. Trump happened to be crossing the street and he stepped off a curb and unintentionally crushed a newly fallen fully formed beautiful blue Robin Egg, the press would hang him for being anti-bird, anti-animal, and uncaring. The corrupt US media is really despicable.

Meanwhile Hillary Clinton can get four Americans with mothers and fathers back home killed in Benghazi and these same bird-life-lovers will not even cover the story. Something is wrong and you know what it is. We all need

Donald Trump and Mike Pence to bring America back to reality and truth.

The country's issues include oppressive taxation; legal and illegal immigrants stealing the best jobs; regulations choking businesses; huge debt and deficits shackling our capital resources; a government Obamacare system that adds taxes and makes health worse; and corporate offshoring, which creates a weaker nation.

Hillary Clinton would have changed none of this because she supports Barack H. Obama's policies, which created the whole mess in the first place.

Additionally, we have a massive energy dependency on our enemies. We redistribute wealth from producers to non-producers. We permit a huge, growing, inefficient government to operate, which continually lies, taxes too much and spends more than it has.

Our government has become enemy # 1 of the people. A good plan, endorsed by Mr. Trump, along with good leaders such as Donald J Trump & Mike Pence is ready to save US from Obama perdition.

It is so great that Donald Trump won the presidency. Can you imagine the negative future of America if we had permitted corruption to continue? When Donald Trump begins to fix the problem-list outlined above, we will be well on our way to making America great again. We can already feel it.

Trump is the Answer

You either love Donald Trump or you hate him. There is little room in-between. I happen to love Trump for the right reasons. I find him to be a gift from God to the American people in our time of great need. After all the weak, wimpy, wobbly conservative leaders, groomed by establishment elitism, who offered little recognition or solution for the concerns of the people; Donald J. Trump, my candidate for president, now my President, is a breath of fresh air.

Thank you to Donald J. Trump for doing the United States a big favor by taking on corruption in both political parties as well as the media. You are doing just fine sir, and my friends and relatives appreciate your taking a hiatus from your wonderful storybook life and using your time to help us. We sure need it.

Though some felt that you were not a viable candidate at the beginning, I was not among their ranks. I saw you grow from day one, when you were introduced to the piranha at the first Republican primary debate. You did very well but nobody would acknowledge you because you were and continue to be the biggest threat to all the establishment elites in both parties that has ever existed. You are especially not liked by the corrupt press because you call them out on their dishonesty. Thank you especially for that. We love it!

You have taken the Republican electorate by storm and I love watching you climbing higher and higher in the polls. We all know the fake news CNN and polls trying to demean your popularity. You are IT Mr. Trump, and we are so glad that on January 20, you arrive for good. You have also won over many Democrats including some in my own family, who switched to Republican just so they could vote for you in the PA primary.

Though the Constitution Party, the Green Party, and the Libertarian Party, and other parties had their own sponsored candidates in the General Election, the importance of this election is well understood by the citizens. Our country is at stake. Thus, I would expect that many of the people in these parties also voted against the status quo to do their part to help make America great again.

I happen to be a lifelong Democrat who is sick of the Democrat Party and the unapologetic corrupt press being against America. At first it seemed unintentional. Now I see it part of a plan to indoctrinate the American people into believing that socialism and communism and Marxist principles are better than American values. For America to remain strong, the Democrats and Hillary Clinton had to be defeated. All citizens of good will joined in to make this happen.

Congratulations are in order for Donald Trump who is a new guy in a tough political scenario. Despite his lack of funding and lack of support, President Trump was able to overtake all the Republicans including the whiners and the long-time establishment elites and he mowed over Hillary Clinton in all but selected areas of the country with a huge population of foreign interlopers.

"Never Trump" Republicans were known in this campaign for taking every dollar the donors would give them to buy support for their now well-known activities against the Trump candidacy. But, it did not work.

How about that great convention and the first class rebuttals to the status quo anti-American speeches during Hillary's convention week? It was heartening to see the Republican campaign rubbing a little Trump moxie onto the major coronation that was supposed to take place at the end of July. The reluctant endorsement by Bernie Sanders and the Debbie Wasserman Schultz firing showed that the Democrats are the Party of chicanery, deceit, and downright cheating. It is nauseating how far to the dark side of the Force, Democratic leadership has gone.

Was it not a wonderful sight for the Trump family to participate in the convention and the campaign for the good of America? It was a pleasure hearing from Melania, Tiffany, Donald Jr., Eric, and Ivanka. What talent!

Please allow a digression for a brief discussion of family talent and how families can do great things together.

My father was one of five Kelly brothers – Ed, Pat, Joe, Mike, & Phil, who were all high-school basketball greats in the 1940's. They formed their own team known as The Kelly Brothers and they played up and down the Wilkes-Barre Wyoming Valley and won their share of many great games against organized teams. Nobody sat on the bench.

It reminds me of the five talent laden Trumps at the convention. It was overwhelming. There is nobody warming the Trump bench because they are all out winning the game—just like the Kelly boys. As an American worried about America, I am appreciative for the Donald Trump candidacy for lending the Five Trumps to the people of the United States during this ever so important campaign for America. Again, it is both heartwarming and very refreshing.

We need every one of the Trump soldiers, especially their leader, who is taking the oath of office for President as I write these words. There is so much corruption, mostly hate-filled biased media speech that Mr. Trump, Mike Pence, and the whole Trump team cannot afford to have anybody out of the contest for long.

The Trump campaign can expect bad stuff to continue--low blows, untruths, unkind assaults, and whatever vile actions the establishment elites, the Democrats, and the corrupt fourth estate choose to unleash.

So, we need all the Trumps, Mike Pence, the Trump campaign team, and we the people at home to continue the fight against the forces of the dark side. Don't believe them. Their purpose is deceit. The truth is a foreign notion to the Hillary people. Now that Donald Trump has won, all Americans have become winners. My sincere thanks to the Trumps et al for taking on the rot in America.

It would be nice for all the Never-Trumpers to reconcile and many have. I think most will come around

The dirty rotten press

The intellectuals of the 18th and 19th centuries, especially Edmund Burke, gave us the notion of Fourth Estate (the press and all other media) as a civil watchdog to keep an eye on those in power. It is very clear from the writing of Thomas Paine and others, who pointed out and also acted upon the idea that we may have just cause to overthrow the state if it is seen to be no longer acting in our interests.

This is not trivial. An unbiased, non-corrupt is essential to the well-being of America. Without violating the Constitution, it would be good to see some laws directed against intentional misrepresentation of facts by the media, which today we call "fake news." The new Justice Department should check the charters of the media to see if lying has somehow made it into their protocols.

The founders were not thinking "hunting," when they explicitly added the Second Amendment to the Bill of Right. Their reasoning is what really drives Americans to actively defend the second amendment. Though hunting with rifles is important, it is not hunting that is the root cause of the drive by patriotic Americans to protect the founders' intention of second Amendment.

There is the possibility and perhaps there is even a likelihood that sometime in the future, scoundrels would take over the government and would need to be dealt a blow that only an armed citizenry could deliver. Finding the very scoundrels who have been driving our country to perdition to be trying as hard as they can to take our guns away make this notion ever more frightening and real.

Today, governments such as ours that make the claim to be acting in the "public interest" must face daily scrutiny of their actions. This is a necessary duty of an alert public in a democratic republic. The government must be called to account when overstepping the bounds of what citizens will support, or when taking actions that are clearly not in our interests. Who knows what President Trump will cover when he pulls the plug and the swamp begins to drain.

Journalism is wanting today

There was a time when the public could rely on journalists and the news media to do this job on our behalf. The separation between the people and the state becomes more important when the economic interests of the powerful establishment elites so frequently dominate society.

In our modern world, the interest of "the nation," can be deduced to be no more than the collective interest of those who wield political and economic power. That of course in 2016 gave rise to the silent revolution that we are still experiencing as the voice of the people has been had all but been snuffed out by the powerful. The people are mad as hell and are not going to take it anymore. Donald J. Trump as our new President gives us all great hope—real hope.

Before January 20th, with the state being represented almost solely by an executive branch of the ruling class, operating with little concern for the Constitution, the people simply could not take it anymore. Hillary Clinton was viewed by good people as preparing to make it even worse. She had to be stopped. Democrats and Republicans who had not voted in thirty years came out to help "Make America Great Again." Now, we are on our way.

I do not like to cast aspersions on anybody but the fact is there is a group known as "low-information voters," who still do not question the spew from the corrupt media. In this election, it was these easily convinced citizens who voted in opposition to Mr. Trump at the behest of the Fourth Estate. Clearly this was corruption at its zenith. Lying and fake news and fake scandals became the norm and those trusting souls who won't look elsewhere for the truth bought the lies and voted in opposition to Trump. Thank God there were not enough of them.

The regular Joes in America were highly motivated as they saw more and more of the "rulers" in both parties stop believing in a government of the people, by the people, and for the people. President Obama who claimed to have been a Constitutional Law Professor had been attacking the Constitution for eight years and he had taken many unlawful actions of which those paying attention were aware. The Constitution has been under assault by our government and we all know that it is this document that gives the people all its rights. That's why I included a copy of the Constitution in Appendix A of this book.

We the people are not willing to settle for a government of the government, by the government and for the government. Unfortunately, before today, January 20, 2017, it would be difficult to tell.

The news media – as the tribune of "the people" – has a major role as the fourth estate to constantly be on guard and alert to actions of the state, particularly when those actions may harm the interests of citizens. In recent years, the fourth estate has mostly been absent, serving as a corrupt wing of the corrupt Democratic Party.

I know in this coming Trump Administration, this will end. It is vital to the interests of American citizens that it end quickly. Let us watch for the weeping and gnashing of teeth as the swamp is drained. It will be a pleasant sound.

Because our long-term foes are also Donald Trump's foes, now that Trump and Pence campaign has changed into the Trump and Pence Presidency, the Trump haters on both sides of the political spectrum – the Bush supporters and Clinton Supporters, seem to have gotten even more vicious. Perhaps seeing their very survival has created a response like a cornered cat.

In response, the good people of America, have aligned with the values brought forth in the Trump campaign and now into the Presidency. We have become less accepting of the outright lies and the plots of subversion because there is simply no room to lose this battle against the dark forces, who for their own selfish interests are determined to keep the country weak, while whining that they really did not lose the election. Rest assured dear Readers, they lost. You can tell they are understanding that on Inauguration day as the intensity of their howling is up many more notches.

It is all about the people deciding to be heard. We are no longer willing to take it anymore, hoping the establishment will find its way. We kicked the establishment out and Donald Trump is now about to pull the plug and drain the swamp. I do love saying that probably as much as you like hearing it.

Donald Trump has given Americans a true hope that our America can once again be God's Country or as noted by President Reagan, a Shining City upon a Hill. This President is already working to Make America Great Again. The times from the recent past when there were glimmers from empty promises that were never fulfilled are over. Americans today are demanding a responsive government as promised by Donald Trump and Mike Pence. We are so pleased that God gave us our victory.

That is why so many of us joined with Donald Trump and the Trump family and the Trump campaign. We have been loyal supporters and now that he is President, we trust that President Trump will keep his word as have presidents of the past such as John Fitzgerald Kennedy and Ronald Wilson Reagan.

I can see that the Five Trumps playing on the first team at the convention believed 100% in the Trump candidacy and they believe in America and they believe in Americans. They also believe in this new Trump Presidency. It is a different kind of Camelot but just like the JFK years, there is something in the air. It is America's turn now to believe in the whole Trump family. I do.

We the people have simply gotten sick of everything being designed for the Republican big shots. We are very tired of the establishment elites such as the George Bushes, Jeb Bush, Carl Rove, Brit Hume, the US Chamber of Commerce, and the many donors who think they can buy America simply by buying its weak, whiny, and wimpy politicians.

Meanwhile Democrats are brewing up one falsehood after another for the corrupt press to spread on an unwary accepting public. More and more members of the public are fighting back and soon will be demanding reforms of the Fourth Estate. How about "The Truth" being one of the big press reforms.

The objective of the press now is to delegitimize the Trump Administration s that Mr. Trump must lead with his hands tied behind his back. They want to finish off the Trump team by telling enough lies that the people finally believe them and acquiesce. This will not happen this time! More and more people have smartened up to the corrupt press and to the corrupt Democrats.

Democrat constituents saw the vile of the dishonest Democratic Party leaders and Hillary Clinton when they destroyed Bernie Sanders in a conspiracy of lies and double-dealing.

A small establishment elite has been running the Republican Party for so long, and rigging the game against the people for so long, that they got caught flat-footed when their old tricks and their "ram it quietly down their throats," tactics simply did not work this time. That is because Donald Trump, the antitheses of the establishment had already entered the arena, and he proceeded to knock the elites over one by one. He is now our President.

The rise of Trump has been a tidal wave. In their deluded minds, the establishment thought they could steal the nomination from Donald Trump and that their strategy would work just the same as it did against Ron Paul in 2012. But Trump has a constituency, which includes you and yours truly and we would not be defeated. We would not stand for it.

I am reminded of Japanese Naval Marshal General Isoroku Yamamoto who, after Pearl Harbor confessed: "I fear all we have done is to awaken a sleeping giant and filled him with a terrible resolve." The attempts of the establishment elites to derail the Trump Campaign were thwarted by a fed-up public. We the public are sick of Republican broken promises. We have lost trust in the Party elite leaders and the donors who no longer care about the people.

Yes, Donald Trump has managed to awaken the silent majority of Americans who previously either did not care or simply did not bother to vote. Some in the past just shrugged their shoulders and accepted that the system is rigged and that all of the little men in the world—all of us insignificant citizens of America, could not have an impact under any circumstances. Trump is the difference. The people rose and would not let negativism affect them. We now have power back in the hands of the people, through President Trump.

Today Donald J. Trump has become a leader for the non-elites. He is the President of all Americans but he knows who has written his Mission Statement. He is for the non-establishment brand of citizen, who simply depends on honest representatives to keep our democratic republic operating smoothly.

President Trump was the perfect alternative to candidates who did the bidding of Bush's and Clintons and their ilk, and who somehow became richer and richer while the ordinary people were becoming poorer and poorer. President Trump was the perfect alternative for leaders who have permitted America herself to be turned into a debt-ridden shadow of its once great self.

Unfortunately, because of elitist propaganda from both Republicans and Democrat members of the establishment, in full cahoots with the corrupt main stream media, the fourth estate, full of journalists that have forgotten American History, Americans are turned off against those willing and eager to promulgate hatred against Donald Trump. Pick on Donald Trump at your own peril. Mr. Trump defends himself well, but we the people must stay by his side as the forces of darkness in American politics try to bring him down.

Unfortunately, because there are some voters who do not have a high information threshold, the Democrats and the Bushes are continuing to drive promote their negative message through the dishonest press. I regret that Bush 41 and Barbara Bush are in the hospital today for the Inauguration. I wish them well. I love the nice note President Bush 41 sent. May it be a sign of goodness for the future.

Too many along the way have accepted the bias towards candidate Donald Trump as if it were true. It is not. That is why I wrote the book: Why Trump? And this book, "… Make America Great Again." President Donald J. Trump is ready to be one of America's best presidents ever. Have you ever seen any President doo so much homework as the President Elect?

Because of the many who are still inundated with negative Trump messages every day, who find it difficult to see the truth, Trump supporters must not be quiet when we are in a group. Instead, like apostles and good disciples of a message to save America, we must refute the lies that are circulating every day. The ham-handed efforts of the Soros crowd to smear Mr. Trump as a racist must be shown to be the lies they are.

Many of our neighbors have found it increasingly difficult to even notice that the democratic foundation of our nation as well as American Sovereignty were being destroyed by the very people who had been conspiring to stop Trump's nomination. They sure don't get the truth from the news. Leaders in the Democratic Party seem to have given up on America and they ease the easily persuaded towards their socialist / communist New World Order.

We who pay attention must be prepared for the assault and do better in helping our friends and neighbors see through the lies. We are making progress for sure as people who would never even use the word Republican in public, have done the unthinkable. They have changed parties so they could vote for Trump in the primary. Let's keep at it. Donald Trump is our new President. Long live the President as he makes America great again.

Chapter 4   The Annual Guest Plan

Fix the border but also save the rest of us

The part of illegal immigration that everybody sees is in our neighborhoods. None of it is behind the gated communities where the CEOS who demand lower wages live, nor is it behind the gates of our esteemed representatives who can't wait to bring in a few more voting Democrats.

As I saw more and more corporations taking jobs offshore, I also saw those corporations that could not leave the country choosing to leave their American workforces behind and with impunity bringing in replacement foreign workers for the Americans who lost their jobs.

Hillary Clinton wanted to remove all impediments to amnesty and the Democratic platform in the last election was hell bent on opening up the borders to bring 'em all down with voter registration cards.

Even before this, President Obama decided the parts of the Constitution with which he did not agree no longer mattered. So, he decided that he could make laws of the ilk that Congress would never approve, and a fully Republican Congress cowered at the very thought that this President might not like them if they acted against him.

Rather than do their jobs, wimpy Republicans feared they would ruin their chances of being reelected until they die. Selfish Congressmen, no representation, and a president who had a big agenda were doing their best together to defeat America and Americans.

That is why early in 2017 a lot of Americans still had not taken down their Christmas trees. Since November 8, the day when President Trump was elected, for many of us, it has been Christmas every day. It is a gift that keeps on giving. The people of this country, who are a big cut above the low-information voters are tickled pink. We know Donald Trump; our new and very welcomed president will not let us down.

Before Trump, whose name can also be HOPE, the people had no hope for the Obama change had placed all hope in the wringer of an old washer and it had been rung dry.

The people were rendered helpless by a wimp Republican establishment and a determined Democratic Party. Democrats were determined to put American employees out of work, replacing them with foreigners. Then, they figured while the Americans were drinking beer at the VFW [the Obama caricature of veterans], they would slip in all these now semi-citizens with documentation that would enable them to vote.

The Republican-dominated Congress had already showed the President he could do anything he wanted so why would these fortified Democrats not go for the gold ring?

For years, only a real dummy could not see the massive illegal immigrations with nobody seeming to be able to speak the American language at K-Mart, Walmart, and all my favorite stores. Americans already knew we had a big problem. Our leaders chose not to make it better and in their self-serving rhetoric promised to make it worse. Then, Candidate Trump began talking about a beautiful wall.

Meanwhile I was figuring we had to do something about 20 to 60 million illegal interlopers living in our neighborhoods, aka, the shadows.

Every problem solution needs a name and so I eventually called my solution to the illegal immigrant problem in the US, The Annual Guest Plan.

I am convinced the plan that I outlined as the Annual Guest Plan is the right plan.

Over time, because Democrats like the idea that the new dependent foreign class will vote Democrat one day, and Republican political elites want so much to please their donor class, who employ these "residents" at sub-minimum wage rates; our government has again intentionally chosen to ignore the wishes of the American people to serve its own massive greed.

The President Trump plan about the wall, would definitely stop the new potential illegal foreign nationals at the border. However, nobody had focused on those illegal residents already in our neighborhoods, aka the shadows, who are beginning to think they own significant parts of America.

Synopsis of Annual Guest Plan

My long-researched solution addresses the 60,000,000 interlopers that snooker Americans officials every day. If an interloper who chooses to be an "annual guest," is well behaved, and we citizens get to define what that means, they will begiven a temporary right to live in America and hold a job for which an American citizen is not competing.

Annual Guests will be 100% out of the shadows and will live like you and I within our neighborhoods, paying for housing as we do. Their kids will go to school and they will pay school taxes like you and me. As part of becoming an annual guest, the former interloper agrees that there will be no more freebies. I mean none.

Thus, to gain their new status, interlopers must promise not to be a burden (defined as costing taxpayers) or they promise to voluntarily deport. The government will help in their deportation and in fact may offer a substantial stipend of $10,000 for those who agree to peacefully go and never come back.

Americans will not pay a dime again for annual guests for education, healthcare or general living. Iron clad identification databases will be built and ID cards with biometrics will be issued and those without such identification will be deported immediately once the program is in full implementation.

EMTALA (what some call free emergency care) will be provided but the annual guest receiver must immediately self deport if the cost of service is not quickly paid or arrangements are not made. An electronic accountability database (EAR) will also be built to keep track of any costs that are not immediately paid by the "annual guest." Unapproved balances mean automatic deportation.

No charge registration first

Annual Guests (AGP) must begin their freedom in the US by registering at no charge at one of many US facilities such as Post Offices. US officials will know all illegal foreign nationals at that point as their status will temporarily be legal.

Under the program, as many as sixty million people must be registered within six months. This is clearly do-able as our national elections are accomplished with many people in just one day. After registering, the former interloper must apply in-person for an annual guest visa and be approved or agree to be deported if they do not apply or do not gain approval for annual guest status.

Since registration is the first act, any interloper who decides to skip the rest of the process will be easy to locate. By then, we will know their addresses.

Americans believe the influx of illegal foreign nationals hurts them and from my own observations, we Americans are 100% correct. With the Annual Guest Plan, Americans are back in charge. The table is turned in this program with the citizen is now holding all the TRUMP cards. AGP's will have no welfare or health benefits other than those provided by their employers. If they seek US benefits, in their application they will have agreed to self-deport.

They will not be able to vote in any election in the US for any office local, municipality, state, or federal. Unless they return to their home country, and begin a process like all others from that country, they can never become a citizen of the US. Under no circumstances as an annual guest member, can they ever vote... ever!

Registration will be free for three months and then for three months it will cost $50.00. After six-months new registrations will be closed forever, and the unregistered and new interlopers will be deported. Those deported who were among the 60 million, will have decided not to accept the olive branch and would have done so at their own peril.

Annual Guest Sign-Ups / Renewals $100.00 / yr.

All registrants must pay $100.00 to apply for annual guest status and go through a vetting process. Renewal will also be $100.00 or a larger fee that recoups administrative costs.

Those granted annual guest status merely have to be well-behaved in order to stay in the US for a lifetime but must renew every year. In year two, three, etc. each annual guest must appear in front of US officials to be vetted again and pay their annual guest fee of $100.

The fee is $100 per year every year unless it costs more to process them. Each year until the plan is proven, each guest must appear before US officials and pay. To repeat, AGP's must make personal appearances once a year to renew and pay their $100.00 and be vetted each year to get their ID cards refreshed.

The details of the Annual Guest Plan are fully revealed in my new book titled President Donald J Trump, Master Builder: The Annual Guest Plan available on both Amazon and Kindle.

The key point is that these people are guests of American citizens. They began as uninvited visitors (interlopers) but this AGP process changes their status. They are not American citizens. They are guests. Once registered and approved, they have a special right granted by the citizens of the US to remain in the US if they are well-behaved, and no longer.

AGPs gain no special privileges. American citizens have all the privileges of citizens in our own country / state.

There are other advanced notions about immigration in the overall plan that may help US officials deal better with the ongoing issue of people wanting to crash into America uninvited for various purposes.

For example, the plan should never cost the US more than if the plan were not in force. Yearly fees would be adjusted as needed to assure there is no taxpayer burden. Illegal foreign nationals who chose to be Annual Guests when granted permission would never be permitted to ever become a burden, financial or otherwise on the citizenry of the USA.

This has been a very light introduction to a very detailed plan. It would be a proper question to ask "Why should America choose to do this?" We could say the answer is "simply because America is a kind nation, and Americans have big hearts." But, there is lots more. We have to solve this problem before it gets even worse.

Americans will be big winners in this plan, and former interlopers will also gain. Of course, the fact that Americans do not want to summarily deport up to 60,000,000 illegal residents overnight is a prime motivator. Americans do not have the stomach to deport 60,000,000 illegal foreign nationals. However, Americans are also sick of paying and are no longer willing to pay the toll for interlopers.

Other benefits of the Annual Guest Plan

Looking at the costs of not having an Annual Guest Plan v having such a plan; it is obvious that there are some special things that can be done to help keep families intact, and these too can cost Americans less; not more.

For example, suppose an anchor citizen through his or her parents could choose to take a $50,000 stipend from the US government to give up anchor citizen status, leave the country and go to his or her home country unimpeded -- with his or her parents. What if the US also provided a nice stipend for the mother and father to be resettled in a safe area of their home country?

They could start anew in their home country with a bankroll and become mini-entrepreneurs in their home country. There may be families who could gain a grub stake as large as $70,000 to several hundred thousand dollars, depending on the # of children to start fresh in their home country with their families intact. Why would they want to stay in America when they have an opportunity to become somebodies in their home countries?

Though some may see this as folly and unaffordable, once a welfare recipient no longer collects welfare, you multiply the annual saving by the number of years that the US would subsidize this family. $50,000 or even a $100,000 would be substantially less cost than supporting a family from birth to death.

The idea of the Annual Guest Plan is to help those stuck in America doing meaningless labor for slave wages. It is also a plan to help Americans subjugated to the effects of a new but clandestine wage scale that comes before all minimum wages, for which they cannot compete.

The cost of interloper services is in the hundreds of billions of dollars and will approach trillions in the coming years. We cannot afford it but we can afford large one-time payments for those willing to set-up shop in their home countries.

Our politicians created this mess so I think it is OK if we help these people get back to their home countries with a grub-stake. We have more than enough reserves to pay for any program that reduces the lifetime burden of an interloper on American taxpayers.

Food for Thought

Frosty Woolridge, a noted philosopher, has a deep perspective on the problem. This quote is from Frosty. It helps all of us get a sense of the reality of the perpetration being played on US taxpayers by our government:

As shown on CBS with Katie Couric this past week, 300,000 pregnant Mexican women cross the border to birth their babies, known as 'anchor babies', in American hospitals at an average cost of $6,000.00 per birth with no complications. If the child suffers heart defects, Downs Syndrome, Autism or any other problems, the costs jump to $500,000.00 with long term care into the millions of dollars. All footed by the America taxpayer!

Not mentioned in Couric's report, that child enjoys free breakfasts and lunches through 13 years of publicly funded education at an average cost of $7,000.00 per year. Additionally, American taxpayers foot the bill for all medical and housing assistance for the child and mother.

More hidden costs add up with ESL classes to teach the child English. Connecticut alone suffers 120 languages in their schools while Colorado suffers over 40 foreign languages that cripple their classrooms.

The list of expenses paid for by American taxpayer soars with time and numbers of illegal aliens. Additionally, legal immigrants sponsor their relatives in chain migration and family reunification at US taxpayer expense.

These immigrants take American jobs while they burn American taxpayer funds for immigrant welfare. This all happens while the US national debt approaches $10 trillion [now $20 trillion]. Immigrants flood into this country while jobs cascade out to China where we owe $1 trillion in T-bills as of 2008. Additionally, we suffer a $700 billion annual trade deficit.

Summary

In summary, I developed the Annual Guest Plan rudiments (AGP) in 2013. I came up with a cute name for it -- The Kelly Plan. I saw all the plans that were out there and no regular Americans, especially those who had been put out of work by the "illegal wage differential," were interested in turning over America to foreigners.

I examined the gang of eight plan, existing law, and other notions about how to solve the nation's problem with too many illegal residents. I found that none of the available solutions addressed all of the issues that having 20 million to 60 million illegal foreign nationals in residence brought to America.

As noted previously, I read the gang of eight plan in 2013, and as you may have noticed in the Preface, I found that it smelled a lot like it was purposely designed to kill America. Why would Republicans John McCain, Jeff Flake, Marco Rubio, and Lyndsay Graham have sold out America in such a harsh way. Rubio lost his opportunities for the Presidential nomination because the people knew he was ready to sell us down the river. Once he went with the GO8, he was out of my mind for good.

No jobs in this scenario would be left for Americans; newly unemployed Americans would have to pay for newly minted citizens; voting in national elections was not ruled out; 33 million more foreign nationals would be invited. It would cost over $6 trillion. It was a terrible deal for the country.

I looked at all of the things that Americans did not like and I looked at what the interlopers liked. I figured out a way to permit well-behaved interlopers to be able to stay in America while giving Americans priorities in all ways. This plan, The Annual Gust Plan, actually will work and it will solve the problem of up to 60,000,000 and it will take a huge financial burden off the backs of Americans.

After such a scintillating introduction, please make sure you read the rest of the plan if you are interested by finding the full book on Amazon or Kindle.

Thank You!

Chapter 5   Saving America: The Trump Way

America is worth saving

The book titled *Saving America: The Trump Way*, written in mid-2016 to help candidate Trump win the election, offers several unique solutions to President Trump to save America from economic ruin. You won't believe how much America needs the solutions in this book until you have gone through the problems and solutions as outlined. We all need Donald Trump and Mike Pence to bring America back from the brink.

Between you and I, it looks like the President and his team have read the book already as many of their ideas run parallel to those exposed in the book.

America has more than one economic issue for sure, but it still is the best place to live on earth. Our nation is full to the brim with economic issues. When tackled one by one, they all can be solved.

The Saving America book shows how to solve the problems that prevent many people in American from having a good life. Donald Trump and Mike Pence have a clear mission to make life better for all Americans. At today's inauguration speech, I saw that President Trump has taken on this challenge.

It seems that all Americans are hunting for jobs. Jobs are posted and there are hundreds of applicants. So, when the people engage the jobs' marketplace with much tolerance, and still find no work, we intrinsically know that it is not our fault. But, that puts no bread on the table.

Today, too much government is the problem. It is mixed into our way of succeeding. It is also in the way of businesses naturally solving their own problems; becoming successful; and hiring lots of people.

A good plan can save US. This book explains the elements of such a plan. Tax and spend will not cut it. Donald Trump as President will go a long way towards a permanent solution

Why would anybody feel compelled to write a book about Saving America? From what? From whom? Is our country in imminent danger?

Depending on how you define imminent, we are in danger and we need an innovative solution to bring us back on the right economic track. In this way, American businesses can begin to do so well that they can again put their "Apply Inside" signs back outside.

From the first moment in June 2015, when he announced, and even before that, I knew and many others knew that Donald Trump is the guy who will make this all work.

So, why did I write this book?
Well, for one thing, he was not yet the President. And, that is a big thing.

Why else did I write this book. It does not take a genius to see that our economy has stopped working. Our financial institutions have been forced to lessen their standards while the taxpayer has become the prop between any of the government's favorite crony-backed businesses (including the banks) and failure.

America is under attack from within and from without. Government has one objective and that is to grow fast so that it can control everything and everybody. Corporations are protecting their assets and their viability from a government gone wild. This new US government will seize whatever it can get from anybody and that includes corporations and their executives.

Government has great ambitions. Tax dollars are the fuel that permits government to grow and prosper. Our government wants more and more and more from people who make less and less and less. On the outside, we have free trade agreements nipping like piranha at all things American, while our own government accepts trade imbalance without a whimper.

It is time to say STOP. All of us together must say STOP to save our country. Electing Donald Trump as our President puts a lot of teeth into the word, STOP! We must STOP runaway government to save our lives. No matter who we are, it is time to STOP the government in its tracks. It is destroying us.

What good will it be even if our side—the side of right and justice wins, if there is nothing left? We need to come together, adopt this plan to save America and fight for America and not for anybody's special interests. It is time America starts winning again. President Donald J. Trump could have written this last paragraph for me.

The book Saving America is about what I have learned and deduced about how Donald Trump can and will make America great again. Along the way, he will save America from the past eight years.

As a professor for over thirty years, whenever I teach a new notion or write a book that teaches different ideas, I want my students to look at things in a different way. Sometimes just a little hint helps somebody entrenched in poor thinking to look on the other side of the boat.

Business students; and I taught in the Business Department of Marywood University for years; are taught to revere business but it should not always be so. For example—corporations, unions, government, taxes, spending, and immigration need to be reined in. But, how

Few business professors would agree with me that a return to Mercantilism principles, and a whole host of other innovative items as one day hopefully will be pushed by Donald Trump to help America survive this major economic slowdown before it melts our country. Most Americans do not know that before the Woodrow Wilson years, the US ran its government on mercantilism and not on an ever-increasing and debilitating personal income tax.

A little bit of mercantilism can go a long way even if we call it a 35% import tax for corporations that build products overseas.Together, we can help make the US a far better country. First of course, we must celebrate that many of us stepped outside our own skins and we elected Donald J.Trump as our president. Bravo America!

Misguided US Economic Policies

When I wrote the reface for Saving America, I posited this important question: "Why would anybody feel compelled to write a book about Saving America? From what? From whom? Is our country in imminent danger?"

I answered it quickly by saying "Depending on how you define imminent, we are in danger, and we need a solution to bring us back on the right economic track so that American businesses can begin to do so well that they put the 'Apply Inside' signs back outside."

Does Donald Trump look like the kind of guy who could ever agree with me. I sure hope so!

A bad economy is a recent phenomenon

Now that Donald J. Trump is the President of the United States, aka POTUS, because he is in this because of his love for America and not for himself, he will get our economy back on track poste haste. Donald Trump, the human being, and Donald Trump, the Executive, does not fail—period. Among many other notions, the Saving America Trump plan would include the following:

- Close Tax loopholes
- Reduce taxes
- Make economy dynamic
- Bring back jobs from China & Mexico
- Pay attention to the debt limit
- Grow the economy at 6% annually by ending inversions
- Cut major unnecessary expenses

- Start cutting government expenses by eliminating the entire EPA & the Dept. of Education
- Secure a 35% boost to economy by eliminating the national debt
- Bring back steel and coal jobs
- Take advantage of US energy resources
- Eliminate & replace economically unsound Obamacare.
- Etc. Etc. Etc.

Economic problems did not show up overnight

The solutions will not be overnight either but once we change direction, with a great new President in charge, you will be able to smell the victory over the economy in the air. Without great leadership—the kind that I am convinced is about to come from a Donald Trump Administration—America would still be suffering from eight years of misguided economic policies. They began in the last two years of the Bush Administration and have carried right through to today. We have been in a ten-year funk.

You may recall that the Republicans lost control of Congress because Bush was perceived by the majority of Democrats to be ineffective against the ills of the day. And, so, the Democrats, two years before Obama became President, swept both houses of Congress and made George Bush a sitting lame duck President.

At the time, regular Joe Americans, never having had to deal with an obviously corrupt press, were encouraged by what they believed to be a truthful media to kick out the Republican Congress even though unemployment was low at 4.6 % and the debt was less than ten trillion.

By the time that the Pelosi led House (They were in charge of the dollars) finished its two years and Bush was on his last Air Force One ride back to Crawford, Texas, unemployment was at 7.3%. The National Debt was over ten trillion dollars and when

Obama became President it began its current trajectory to just about $twenty trillion.

On the way to today, during the Obama Presidency, the unemployment rate went over 11% and the doctored rate tapered off for about a year to just over 8% and now it hovers around 5%. Honest economists will admit that the Obama numbers are fraudulent as more people ae unemployed than in the country's history.

Additionally, few who lost their jobs found a new job with comparable earnings power and most found no job at all. Yet, President Obama and the Democrat controlled media were able to take victory lacks about how they had tamed the economy while nobody could get a job. You figure that one out!

The Obama Department of labor owed their jobs to guess how, "Obama" So, it was no surprise when Obama's Department of Labor figured out a way to not count those unemployed longer than six months in his unemployment statistics. They were still unemployed, but they did not count. This was done so the president would be able to brag about his fudged numbers to an unwary and for a long time, adoring public. Only those who checked their brains at the doors believe that today.

Nonetheless, things are not good in the USA today as more people are out of work than ever before. This is like a state of the state as Donald Trump will quickly put a dent in this morass. The debt right now as former President Obama is being helicoptered around Washington on his way to Palm Springs, is just about twenty trillion and it is climbing fast with no end in sight.

Other than a big-time bankruptcy crash, the timing of which is uncertain, there is little positive in the country's economic future other than the mind of our new President. This is not to say that this is not a big deal! President Donald Trump is now the brightest light on the scene with a major promise to make America great again. It was up to the voters such as you and I to give him the opportunity to help us. I am so glad we did!

They say that when your neighbor is out of work, it is a recession and when you are out of work it is a depression. Right now, I know that I am out of a job and a number of my neighbors are out of a job. I was fired by the University where I taught when I ran for Congress against a Democrat incumbent who had sent a lot of dollars to the institution. After top-level evaluations as a professor at the university for years, I was replaced by a foreigner on a Visa from the University of Egypt. No kidding. I got over it. You are reading one of the products of my recovery.

My one neighbor had a great job with the city but a new Mayor ended it for him. There are other stories out there but the job loss is still too real. I know. My neighbors know. Many Americans know. Even low-paying Call Center jobs locally have about fifty to one hundred applicants for each job. Let's just say that things are not good and it has been almost ten years since anything good has happened positively in our economy. I really believe Donald Trump when he says he will change that.

So, while sitting in my man cave, thinking through the kind of things people in man caves think about; my first thoughts were about what could have initially made it so bad for Americans.

After I had mulled that for a while, I spent a lot more time figuring out how to solve the problem by putting a great plan into the hands of a great leader. I have solved the problem on paper in my book, Saving America. You now have the essence of the presentation in your hands right now and you can get the whole book by checking out amazon.com/author/brianwkelly. Scroll until you find the book you want.

If the notions outlined in the Saving America book are implemented as described, our economic problems will be solved, and they will be solved very quickly. In 2012, when I wrote the first version of this book, nobody in government had the guts to implement this plan even though they knew it would work.

Donald Trump is a different kind of leader... Finally! A lot of us are using prayer and we have our fingers crossed as a backup hoping that Mr. Trump lives a long-time on Pennsylvania Avenue or Trump Towers as President. Finally, a good American is making great decisions in the Oval Office.

So, let's ask ourselves what US economic problems are there that are so compelling that I would feel the need to devise a solution for them and then write a book about the solution so that others can see that the problems, though complex, are all solvable?

Before we explore solutions, let's take a broad brush look at what is haunting the US and why the economy has been at the bottom level and why there are no good jobs left for regular Americans in the private sector.

Let me offer the quick answer first as to why.

The reason there are no real jobs to speak about other than those that on the average have cut the American middle class average wage by $5,000.00 in the last five years is simple to answer. The answer is: "The economy is bad." Yes; it is obvious but that is not a joke.

Why is the economy so bad after almost eight years of a President Obama regime that claims the economy is great? The Obama Administration has no problem lying.

Obama and company were supposedly trying to make the economy better? But, they tried to use government to solve the problem. The Obama eight years is one of those times that if there were no government, things would have gotten better by themselves.

Said differently "this is one of those times that if there were no Barack Hussein Obama trying to make things better, things would have gotten better by themselves.

There are lots of specific issues that cause America to be in a state of economic malaise. Let me talk about a few of them generally before we move on to the specific solutions in this chapter about a How-To Book about "Saving America The Trump Way—it included tips from Donald Trump.

Well, if you are fortunate enough to have a job, then you know that there are oppressive taxes that continue to stifle individual, national, and business creativity. If you are a business owner, you are frustrated because whenever you peek your head out of the company looking for a solution, the government plays a game of whack-a-mole with your head. After licking your wounds, you pick yourself up and try again but the prospects of success with the Obama-regime were not very hopeful. Things have changed.

If you are a college graduate or you have an MBA or PhD, you may have found that just like me, legal immigrants are being hired before you for the few skilled academic jobs available. If you are a high school grad or a working mom without college skills, you may have already found that Americans need not apply. Cheap labor is plentiful. "We do not need you Americans."

Small businesses have found government-created sustenance-choking business regulations that put them on a cliff riding a teeter totter—not sure which way the wind will blow. Come on, wasn't that a great sentence?

People have found more and more personal liberty & freedom being stolen by the government and though I do not understand it, there are still many who could not find it in their hearts to blame the current Obama Administration—yet he and his goons were the perpetrators.

Their love affair with President Obama endures after his exodus, plane left free ride to Palm Springs CA, while they use their access cards for food and necessities.

China is Kind?

The government is spending money from China creating major deficits and adding to a huge national debt that has put the United States on the brink of bankruptcy. Donald Trump is on record saying that "if our debt reaches $24 Trillion, we are toast!" Amen! Right now, we are just under $20 Trillion climbing at a $trillion per year under Obama.

And, yes, the big healthcare takeover added huge taxes, which are a big burden on businesses. The people now pay more for health insurance than ever before in their lives. Obamacare was a lie in the first place. Ist intention was not better health care. It was to give government more control over the people. Over 1/6 of the economy has to do with healthcare, and government wants full control.

Perhaps after the Palm Springs vacation the former President and Michelle will come back and the former POTUS will become the unofficial Miffintiff of US Healthcare. The same goofs that donated for Hillary could keep him operating as the King of Healthcare for years. Who knows?

Plus, as most already know there was never an attempt in the Obama regime to limit spending. There is more government spending than ever and the experts say for all that, our health and our healthcare has gotten worse. Meanwhile the crony friends of government officials are making millions from our misery simply because they are friends of the former POTUS.

Is Trump inheriting a strong nation?

You may know that the US is now classified as a de-industrialized (i.e. weaker) nation because our manufacturing is done overseas.

Offshoring has stolen the best American jobs and nobody knows how to bring them back. Donald Trump actually seems to know how and he began exploring how, even before his inauguration. is Worse than that, nobody in the Obama government ever tried. In his nomination acceptance speech, Donald Trump promised that those days are over. America First! Amen!

Donald Trump and the rest of us know that American Corporations left town over the last thirty years to make their products where wages are theoretically cheaper and taxes are lower. They come back often, however, to sell their products.

They build their wares offshore and they bring those products back to America and pay no tribute to our country for the right to do business here. This really annoys President Trump but it annoyed Americans long before he was elected. It is time to no tlisten to corporate rhetoric but instead collect a mercantile fee for no behaving American.

The public cost of moving jobs offshore

When the corporations left town, they paid nothing to the US for the trauma they caused in moving the jobs offshore. They just left and they continue to leave whole towns which become unemployed.

Yet, because of what must be big government corruption at many levels, they are not charged with crimes and are not asked to reimburse the tax funded unemployment compensation expense for their callous actions. Donald Trump will end this crap.

America is left without the jobs and then American taxpayers must pay the unemployment claims of those left behind. Meanwhile, the establishment and corporate fat cats make more money and show their middle fingers to America and Americans.

Energy in America produces jobs

Though we have tons of energy right here in this country and on our shores, government insists that we keep doing business with dirty, nasty, unfriendly enemies of the US rather than drill here and now. Hillary and Obama both vowed to put the coal mines in the US out of business while China is energizing its economy on coal and their economy is now doing better than ours. Thank God neither is in power now.

Our government under Obama and Bush before him has been more interested in splitting up a pie that wage-earners provide and giving a big share of that pie to non-wage earners. They can't get it that people are opposed to such redistribution.

They don't understand that the right way is to stoke the economy to create a much larger pie simply by using sound economic principles designed to work. Donald Trump, an accomplished businessman knows this is a recipe for disaster and he knows how to fix it and make America great again! He now has his chance and success is just around the corner.

The government as an entity however, wants the takers in our economy to depend more on government and vote for the Party that gave them their last free dollar. The truth is that for those Americans on the take, the state of the economy does not seem to matter to them. Work opportunities do not matter. They get their cash and sustenance from the government. Trump, with my blessings and yours, will end this.

People on the take cannot and do not feel very good about themselves as they become unproductive members of society. However, the Obama Administration has trained them to suck it in and believe that it is better to feel worthless and depressed and have their access card than to have a nice paying job with five times earnings and a smile for the opportunities and successes in life for them and their offspring.

Government feeds an unwary population with propaganda so that those people will simply accept government as a master. Paying these people to do nothing is a big drain on our economy and it results in higher taxes for all of us. Government also seems to enjoy lying to its citizens much more than telling the truth.

Government is massive and dysfunctional. It lines up against the people. Yet, somehow, no matter how many times our leaders mess up, they are willing to make the same mistakes again because a Luddite following will re-elect them anyway.

We can do a lot better than this. After Trump's Inaugural speech I am convinced that the sky is the limit. What we need is a "unique," plan for economic recovery and job creation with no BS. We need a Trump plan that puts Americans first in all ways.

We need a plan that straightens out the tax mess but also reaches into critical areas that are impeding economic growth today such as regulations, immigration, and excessive taxation and excessive spending.

Additionally, we need a plan that alters our pure capitalism system into one that is more mercantilist (Helps capitalism be successful). Mercantilism provided the economic engine for the country when the founders were in charge.

Jobs are hard to come by anywhere in the world today including the United States. Even some political liberal progressives who want to be reelected are starting to say that "you can blame the government for that." In this day and age, you can blame the government for lots more than that, and nobody would think that you were kidding.

Despite no jobs for anybody else, the number of US government employees is growing at blinding speed. Federal and state employees are gaining jobs at a record pace. This is not part of anybody's economic solution.

This is a big part of the problem. Donald Trump is already tuned in and I expect to see a hollowing of what once was seen as essential government programs. The only essential part of most of these programs is that nobody knows what they are for and so they are deemed essential by default.

While government grows, there is less and less real work even for government workers. And, so many agencies, even those that originally did good work in their functionary role as well as their advisory role to the President and Congress, have branched into areas that now hurt the economy rather than help it.

The more government employees (other than the military) that are collecting paychecks, the greater the drag on private sector jobs and the economy as a whole. We can do lots better! Donald Trump should axe out whole departments.

Why did I write "Saving America?"

I keep saying this same spiel because most people either do not get it or they cannot remember it. Anybody paying attention knows that our economy has stopped working. Our financial institutions have been forced to lessen their standards while the taxpayer has become the prop between any of government's favorite crony-backed businesses (including the banks) and failure. The United States once represented rugged individualism in all we did and only the strong survived. Now, people pound their chests and claim to be weak so that the Community Chest gives them more hot dogs than their neighbors.

America became the strongest of nations because of a philosophy that says America and Americans are the best, period. Yet, our government today seems like it is against strength as it attempts, through socialistic, progressive, and Marxist principles to create a society of wimps, in which the American dream is little more than a government handout.

America is under attack from within and from without. Government has one objective and that is to grow so that it can control everything and everybody. Corporations are protecting their assets and their viability from a government that would seize whatever it can get from anybody and that includes corporations and their executives.

Government has great ambitions. Dollars are the fuel that permits government to grow and prosper. Our government wants more and more and more from people who make less and less and less. On the outside, we have free trade agreements nipping like piranha at all things American, while our own government accepts trade imbalance without a whimper.

Chapter 6   RRRRRR The Trump Way

Reduce, Repeal, Reindustrialize, Raise, Revitalize, Remember

The full set of R's in the RRRRRR Trump Way is as follows:

1. Reduce Taxes
2. Reduce Immigration
3. Reduce Regulations
4. Reduce Spending
5. Repeal Obamacare
6. Reindustrialize America
7. Reduce Offshoring
8. Raise Tariffs
9. Revitalize Energy
10. Reduce Redistribution
11. Reduce & Eliminate Lying
12. Reduce Government
13. Remember Mistakes…

Now that he is President, Donald Trump is the designated best man in America to design and shepherd the country's recovery. Several years before he was a candidate, I wrote a book simply called RRR, and then when he was in his prime during Summer 2016, I revised the book substantially and retitled it RRRRRR: The Trump Way and I made it part of the eleven book Trump Way Series on Amazon. Ten of the books are featured within.

I still call the plan RRR, which today is short for RRRRRR. It is a code word for a lot of things and it gives the same positive feeling as former Presidential candidate Herman Cain's presentation of his 999 plan. When we developed the top three bullets for this recovery plan, all noticed that all three verbs began with the word reduce.

From this simple observation, the RRR plan was conceived. Along the way to a full set of issues and solutions, there are an additional three sets of 3 R's that are also fleshed out in the RRRRRR book.

Like the book, Saving America, but a little more specific. The RRRRRR plan has the big bullets to make America great again. It's not that America is not great, it's that its greatness has been reduced for eight long years and it needs an uplifting. That's where President Trump comes in.

He knows that our economy has stopped working. Our financial institutions have been forced to lessen their standards while the taxpayer has become the prop between any of government's favorite businesses and failure.

The United States once represented rugged individualism in all we did and only the strong survived. America became the strongest of nations because of that "manly" philosophy. Our government today seems like it is against strength as it attempts, through socialistic, progressive, and Marxist principles to create a society of wimps, in which the American dream can be little more than a handout.

President Donald Trump is already beginning to change that as he rekindles America's greatness using the Trump RRR Way!

Like many other conservatives who supported Herman Cain, I have always liked the ring of the former Presidential candidate's presentation of his 999 plan. As noted previously, when I had developed my own top three bullets when I ran for the US Senate against Robert P. Casey Jr. in Pennsylvania in the fall

2011, I noticed that all three points began with the word reduce. On this day, my version of the RRR plan was conceived. Donald Trump as a candidate already talking about most of the R's in this plan, in one way or another, and they are very plentiful in the plan that we formally called RRRRRR, the Trump Way when we refreshed it in Summer 2016.

If EF Hutton were to take a look at Donald Trump's career in business, he would say that Mr. Trump, a well-known Billionaire gained his money the old-fashioned way. "He earned it!" Trump knows business and he will run the US as a business. I am hoping that he notices all of the bells and whistles of the RRR plan and the president adopts the basic principles of the RRR plan to move America towards its destiny of long-term greatness.

President Trump to Make America Great Again using RRRRRR."

Proud and Patriotic Americans were well impressed by the many connected themes of Donald Trump's campaign. We've all heard them many times before the inauguration and we continue to hear them as the president is on a mission to make them all happen.

Make America Work Again! Make America Smart Again! Make America Strong Again! Make America Proud Again! Make America Safe Again!—and of course the big one: Make America Great Again!

When the soon-to-be President-addressed the American Legion in September, 2016, he minced no words about his plans to turn the country around from its current malaise caused by a life-threatening case of progressive socialism-liberalism disease. Among other things, Candidate Trump said:

" When I am President, I am going to look at every trade deal we have across the world and see what steps must be taken to protect American jobs and create new opportunities for American workers. We will fight for every last American job.

"We're going to show ourselves and the world again what a strong and growing American economy looks like.

"We are going to give major tax relief to every worker and small business in this country, bring thousands of new companies and millions of new jobs back to our shores – and unleash an American Energy Revolution."

He was not kidding. We are on our way!

Hillary Clinton's plan of course would have strengthened the disease and would have weakened the antibodies that great people like President Trump have created to fight this paralyzing epidemic.

Ladies and Gentlemen, there are a lot of R's in those three short paragraphs from a much longer Donald Trump speech to the American Legion. RRRRRR.

Unlike the Herman Cain plan, the RRRRRR focuses on many more areas that need to be addressed to turn around our economy and stimulate job creation. Cain's 999 plan addressed a major change in the tax structure. The RRRRRR plan, on the other hand includes taxes but it reaches into critical areas that are impeding economic growth today such as regulations, immigration, and spending.

Additionally, the RRRRRR plan suggests that we alter our pure capitalism system into one that is based on capitalism but is more mercantilist than the present approach.

From right after the Bush years, Jobs have been hard to come by anywhere in the world today including the United States. Even some liberals were beginning to say that "you can blame the government for that." In this day and age, you can blame the government for lots more than that, and nobody would think you were kidding.

Despite no jobs for anybody else, the number of US government employees is growing at a record pace. This is not part of the solution. A burgeoning government work force is a big problem. While government grows, there is less and less real work even for government workers.

And, so many agencies, even those that originally did good work in their functionary role as well as their advisory role to the President, have branched into areas that now hurt the economy rather than help it. The more of them there are unfortunately, the greater the drag on private sector jobs and the economy.

I revised another book recently about eliminating the EPA. Of all the agencies gone wild under Obama, the EPA is # 1. It is the poster child for government agencies gone crazy The EPA creates more regulations than any other agency and none are good for America.

There is an R in RRRRRR, the mission of which is to Reduce Regulations. The EPA was not created to become bad. However, it was not too long after the EPA's inception that it became a monster in both and in its intrusive tactics. The typical victims of the EPA have been small businesses, small farms, and regular people who are caught up fighting ridiculous EPA regulations of private property to keep their business afloat.

Small business people and small landholders wanting to use their private property do not have the legal staff to withstand the continual onslaught from the EPA. Everyday people have been affected indirectly through increased costs, but recently with the

Light Bulb act, and other silly yet intrusive measures the EPA even terrorizes US households.

The EPA threats to close power plants must be taken seriously. Coal fired plants are necessary for those in the north to heat their homes and for everybody to have lights. President Trump will stop the nonsense and turn over necessary EPA functions to the states and reduce choking regulations on us all.

Helping the President get the job, Former Oklahoma Attorney General Scott Pruitt is President Donald Trump's choice for Environmental Protection Agency administrator. He will help the President make America great again by getting rid of burdensome regulations and turning a lot of the EPA functions over to the states.

Pruitt comes to the job with great qualifications and a good record as the AG of Oklahoma. Trump chose Pruitt because he was the best of a bunch of great candidates. It is a great appointment for Americans because like myself, proud author of Kill the EPA, Pruitt is a fierce EPA critic and rightfully so. He has sued the agency over its regulations of power plants. The AG of too many states are finding it necessary to tangle with the Obama Feds. Those days are gone.

Pruitt's appointment is certainly a great signal for Americans that the Trump administration is intent on reversing President Barack Obama's moves to curb the climate change emphasis.

EPA regulations are serious and this is a serious book. If the EPA caused issues are not addressed with an all-inclusive plan such as RRRRR, and the major changes in philosophies that are necessary to bring our problems under control are not considered, we would have little reason to expect improvement. President Trump is very serious about making America great again! He has a lot of R's in his bag of tricks

Businesses have obviously decided that the US regulation and tax nightmare is not worth their effort anymore. For PR reasons, of course, they are not telling anyone that. They simply don't want to deal with high taxation, oppressive regulations, and a government that is more pro-union than pro-people or pro-industry. Despite government's official stance, Obama's team were more than complicit in helping business execute its destructive plans to rid the US of major industry and suffer no consequences.

The RRR plan addresses all the sticky areas where corruption reins and corporations have been able to undermine what is good for America and Americans. The RRR plan is good for the economy. It is good for the people. It is good for jobs. And, for those corporations that want to sign up to be American-centric, it is good for corporations.

It is the solution balm that offers a gutsy, unique, real, and workable path to get America back on its feet. There is nothing like it anywhere else. All we need is the resolve for the RRR plan to make us successful. President Trump will assure its success.

America is under attack from within and from without. Government has one objective and that is to grow so that it can control everything and everybody. Corporations are protecting their assets and their viability from a government that would seize whatever it can get from anybody and that includes corporations and their executives. Government has great ambitions.

Dollars are the fuel that permits government to grow and prosper. Our government wants more and more and more from people who make less and less and less. On the outside, we have free trade agreements nipping like piranha at all things American, while our own government accepts trade imbalance without a whimper. Donald Trump will not permit America to be second to any other nation.

Unions help a small percentage of the population and elevate their life style above all others. If 100% of the population were unionized, we all know that unions would become completely ineffective.

The people, who do not work for the government or who do not belong to unions are the ones being squeezed most by this economic malaise with dollars being printed on the presses of the US Mint as fast as the paper can be shipped in. The inflationary effects on the poor are worse than any flat tax system you can imagine.

The first time I mentioned the RRR Jobs Plan for America, was on an afternoon at the Barney Inn, Wilkes-Barre on October 21, 2011. I announced that I was running for the US Senate.

The RRR plan, aka RRRRRR The Trump Way, is a way of bringing all of the facets of a robust recovery together in a way that can be remembered easily by all Americans After I had concluded my Barney Inn Speech with the Pledge of Allegiance, including that 60+ year old phrase, "under God," and I waited patiently for the applause of my friends and relatives (they had no choice) to cease, there was a round of questions from the press.

The three R's traditionally have been about education and how important it is to learn Reading, Writing, and Arithmetic when you are young. But, Trump's three R's are not about education. The three R's are a unique economic and jobs plan for America.

RRR is a simple to understand yet comprehensive solution that can very quickly change the economic and jobs picture into results that include Americans of all ages having the opportunity to go to work again. Let's look at the R's again. The three main R's in this plan are

- Reduce taxes
- Reduce immigration
- Reduce regulations.

There are three other sets of 3 Rs that round out the RRR plan and make it very comprehensive compared to anything else that is circulating. Besides, with all these R's, you can bet this plan will work:

Set 2
- Reduce Spending
- Repeal Obamacare
- Reindustrialize America

Set 3
- Reduce Offshoring
- Raise Tariffs
- Revitalize Energy

Set 4
- Reduce Redistribution
- Reduce / Eliminate Lying
- Reduce Government & Remember Mistakes

The Trump RRRRRR plan is easy to remember, and it will be easy to implement if Congress has the political will to abandon lobbyist and other special interest demands and it chooses to address the needs of American citizens. The plan is all we need to make America successful again. When President Trump puts forth RRRRRR, the Congress will not be able to say "no."

There are those who suggest that an approach such as the RRR plan will take a long while to be effective as the impetus for tariffs and taxes to cause a change in corporate behavior will not come overnight. These are the same people who thirty years ago said it is no use drilling more in the US to solve the short-term energy problem because it would take more than ten years to begin seeing results.

We have had three times ten years to do the right thing on energy and we did not do it because it would take too long. Yet, if we had addressed the problem thirty years ago, we would not have the problem today.

The RRR plan is structured to show positive results immediately and continue to get better until it is all implemented. That ten-year figure seems to be back however, by the naysayers.

We the people have a major role in making the US a far better country. Together with President Donald J. Trump, we will make America Great Again!

Eight guiding principles for RRRRRR

The detailed raw ideas for the eight guiding principles of the RRR plan from the book are shown below. President Trump has been leading with these right from June 2015, when he announced his candidacy. Now it is time to make it all happen. Here are these great eight notions:

1. Americans First. This movement is about American Jobs, border security, the border wall, border security, border fences, and states' rights.

We must shut down excessive legal and all illegal immigration. Many already know that over 2.2 million legal aliens get jobs each year in the US? Let's first reduce this to .2 (point 2) before the President declares a moratorium.

Reward businesses that hire Americans. There should be no tax breaks for companies that choose to offshore jobs. Moreover, there should be a huge unemployment tax on companies found using illegal labor. They should pay for the unemployed.

There needs to be a stiff import tax on Chinese goods, especially those goods produced overseas by any American corporation. Just watch the jobs come back.

Since American corporations take so many American jobs overseas, President Trump needs to invite the businesses in other countries to set up plants in America, and give Americans those new jobs in America.

It should also be OK when foreign companies manufacturing in America take the business from so-called American corporations. Let's support corporations that love America and who give Americans Jobs. Let the others, those corporations that once acted American—let's let them sell their stuff overseas.

2. America needs fiscally conservative principles in action. Government needs to govern and not pick winners and losers in business and no more crony capitalism. There should be no bailouts; no takeovers; no porkulus adventures; and no government takeovers of businesses.

We need a balanced budget amendment. Glass Steagall should be reinstituted and the Community Reinvestment Act (CRA) should be abolished as it hurts Americans and our institutions Dodd / Frank and Obamacare must be repealed. There should not be a replacement as government should exit the Health Business completely.

The cure has been worse than the cause. If we believe that those receiving subsidies on Obamacare deserve free health insurance than adjust Medicaid levels to include them. Medicaid already is a well-functioning program to help the poor gain medical care.

Also, the federal government needs to support EMTALA – The Emergency Medical Treatment and Labor Act (EMTALA) is a federal law that requires anyone coming to an emergency department to be stabilized and treated, regardless of their insurance status or ability to pay. This is the emergency health care we all need at some time.

3. Respect Life: On the pro-life, we must believe that human life begins at conception. Dr. Alveda King, the niece of the great Martin Luther King can give us all a lesson on Women's rights. She called out the January 21 Women's' March as missing the opportunity to work for women's rights. She asked why pro-life women are not looked on by the Women's March as women. She also asked how women could be free when baby women in the womb are unprotected and permitted to be slaughtered.

In her own writings, King has compared the anti-abortion movement to the abolition and Civil Rights movements of the past, reminding her readers that although abortion hasn't ended as quickly as many Americans may have hoped, "Rome wasn't built in a day"–and those who are pro-life must "unify and keep moving forward." Women who want to kill little women in the womb do not help the cause of women. They hurt women and the cause.

4. Reduce taxes to stimulate the economy by restructuring or eliminating the monster IRS tax system. The John F. Kennedy style needs to be used for rates if the current system is used. However, it would be great if we could migrate to a FAIR Tax and eliminate the IRS and the corporate income tax at the same time. Herman Cain's 9, 9, 9 was a good plan and it had a nice ring, especially when Herman said it.

Without the Fair Tax, we must reduce or eliminate the corporate tax. Tariffs need to be reintroduced in the form of early US mercantilism to help reindustrialize the US. This will give US companies a reason to build products in mainland USA. Offshoring companies should get no corporate breaks. Companies that hire illegals should get zero tax breaks

5. A smaller government will pay huge dividends to America and Americans. After all we pay all the people in this expanding government huge salaries. Ron Paul, a great baby doctor and a great Congressman has spoken out that government agencies are unconstitutional. Only Congress can make laws, not bureaucrats. He's right. Eliminating harmful, costly agencies such as the EPA, FDA, USDA, Interior, Energy, Education, will all help make America great again.

6. Government needs to be transparent, accountable, and open. There should be no closed doors. All Obama czars must be fired post haste. Fire all czars.

In December, 2009, to alert conservatives to the perpetration by President Obama, NewsMax's David A. Patten wrote a telling piece about the forty-four faces of "Czars." The title boldly appeared on the cover of NewsMax.

David A. Patten's article, "All the President's Czars" including the skinny on who the Czars were and Patten looked upon their dossiers as m as glimpses of "Who's Who Among Obama's Special Assistants." To say the least, it was very interesting and eye-opening.

Whereas, the Democrats today are busting President Trump on his cabinet nominations, these people had no official status. Most went on to the czar-dom with no Senate confirmation. Most had huge salaries, earning well into six figures. The people had no way of affecting their movements as they were accountable only to the president.

As an example of Executive largesse, the Eurasian Energy Czar earns over $400,000, which is Obama's salary. Most came with extreme political viewpoints, reflecting "a distinct tilt to the left." It was far easier for Obama to get bad regulations in on the people with a staff that was unanswerable even to cabinet appointees.

Ironically, the former president had when he became president that he would, "reverse the biggest problem of George W. Bush, trying to bring more and more power into the Executive Branch and not go through Congress." He never did. He surrounded himself with unaccountable czars who were activists for Obama's ideology.

Patten said: "I say his biggest problem, outside of ignoring God, is Valerie Jarrett, a Muslim, exercising her "extraordinary influence." Her "Czar-like" title, "Senior Advisor and Assistant to the President" could be why he's so protective, sympathetic, empathetic towards Muslims. What happens to the czars when Obama's gone? Can't wait to see. Maybe some are gone already like Van Jones {who was forced out early}.

7. The US must remain pro-Israel. Israel is our only friend in the Middle East. Barack H. Obama was confused o he permitted his ideology to get the best of him. President Trump knows that Israel is the only friend of good countries across the world within the Middle East. Despite the disrespect the former President showed to Israel. Israel has remained the only real friend of the US in the Middle East, despite the "Arab Spring."

There are some other groups who are looking at the background of the changing reality in the Middle East.

There is still the possible establishment of an independent Kurdish state, and it might be good and it might be bad. One of the leaders of the Kurds offered this quote: "The Turks support the wrong side," he says, and insists on making it absolutely clear that the fight against ISIS will take a long time."

It helps to understand Israel and its relationship by knowing that the first prime minister, worldwide, who supported Kurdish independence was Benjamin Netanyahu, the Prime Minister of Israel. "We are grateful for what he said and for what Israel did. It is a model for the Kurds," says the Kurdish leader. "The Kurds have no other friends in the Middle East except Israel. We know that for the security of the coming generations we have to cooperate and work together against terrorism.

For its own reasons, the Obama Administration placed a big wedge between the US and Israel. What do the Kurds know that the US does not? -- Was it just Obama and his ideology or was it something deeper like religion? Who knows. Obama is gone, thank God. President Trump knows that Israel is a friend of the US.

8. US needs a Strong Defense— "Speak softly and carry a big stick," The US should not go starting wars. However, we should win by a mile in all wars in which we engage. Use big drones and micro-drones; few foot soldiers. We have 8000 or more drones & $5 Billion in budget. We should use our resources and our technology--not American blood. We also always need an exit strategy -- get out quickly with a win. Send in the drone dragonflies. It will seem like one of the 10 plagues. Why can't we win.

President Trump says we will "knock ISIS off the face of the earth." Let's do it smartly and not waste American life with rules of engagement that put our troops in more danger than the real dangers which they face.

Wiping out ISIS will help make America great again for sure.

9. Tame the Lying Media Though not one of the original eight guiding principles, this is very important. Americans know that the pompous, biased news media is anti-American. Despite the founders knowing a fourth estate, a patriotic honest press was needed, the US media complex ruled by powerful corrupt corporations stopped telling the truth years ago, about things they do not believe.

These folks do their best to help the dark side of life as much as they can. Most of the media live in gated communities so they do not see firsthand the impact of illegal immigration and many other ills which they champion. Yet, too many Americans believe the media is reporting facts, instead of the drivel they provide.

A few media lies, here and there, can go a long way in helping Americans believe there is no issue with immigration and other issues. The media lies. They lied about Donald Trump's candidacy and they continue to lied about his presidency. There must be a way to force the media to do its job of reporting truth, not opinion of truth. If the media is really a political organization, it should be characterized as such.

Even while putting the bones back in the soup to get a second batch of broth is becoming a retro means of survival, good Americans do not want to blame others who also are suffering. Yet, Americans know well that the media has no such scruples. Thankfully, President Trump is taking them on and should as they represent the Democrat Party who were soundly defeated on November 8, 2017 by President Donald J. Trump.

Chapter 7 Jobs! Jobs! Jobs! The Trump Way

Where Did The Jobs Go? How Can We Get Them Back?

If you are out hunting for a job, you better be carrying a scattergun because jobs are plain and simple hard to find and hard to get in the sights. I know you won't be using a Purdey "shotgun," which is the best, even if you are job hunting. That's because, if you are unemployed and you have $100,000 to spend on a house or a gun, I'll bet that you would take living indoors over having the best job hunting shotgun in the marketplace. Too bad it was not that easy. Maybe it is as I am convinced that President Donald J. Trump knows how to solve everybody's job problem.

Jobs are hard to come by and you can blame the government for that. In twelve essays in the book titled as *Jobs! Jobs! Jobs! The Trump Way*, released in 2016, we discuss Jobs! Jobs! Jobs!. We'll tell you where they have gone in this book and how to bring those rascals back. And, folks, we plan to bring those Jobs back alive. President Donald Trump is our man in charge of getting the job of jobs done! He was the only presidential candidate ever who hired a person for a private sector job! Wow! Now, he is going to help businesses of all kinds do the same.

Obama – The anti-jobs president

Most Americans are aware of the major battle that had been going on from day one of Obama times until March 21, 2010 when Obamacare passed. This was the very first reason for why nobody in the administration did anything but pay lip service to the Jobs! Jobs! Jobs! problem.

There is some good news as we are now just about to move into post Obamacare times. The new President, Donald J. Trump and new candidates for Congress from both parties have planned to repeal and remake healthcare legislation so it will not bankrupt America. Of course, my recommendation is that there be no replacement and those deemed too poor to afford Obamacare (taking subsidies) be put on Medicaid at least temporarily until it all gets sorted out.

Now that the new Congress and the new President are sworn in, it should not be too long from now that Obamacare is history— the sooner the better. We have been stuck with Obamacare for far too long.

The irony in all this is especially in a book about Jobs! Jobs! Jobs! that the single biggest jobs killer that passed in the 111th Congress was Obamacare. And it passed during a period in which President Barack Hussein Obama had just promised that he was done with his healthcare agenda and he was going to concentrate on Jobs! Jobs! Jobs! Hah! It was just a lie.

How can you tell if a politician is lying? "Their lips are moving." Obama became the salesman in chief for Obamacare even after its passage and had little time for anything but his image from then on. The fact is that he had little time for Jobs because he was doing his job as prevaricator in chief. But what about his promises? To be kind, we can say his promises were simply prevarications.

Media critics from the past have said that W. C. Fields was so good at lying and kidding and joking that he made prevarication into an art form. The former President clearly is an artist.

On the Web, all things are possible. That's not necessarily a lie but it is an exaggeration. When I went to find the exact meaning of prevarication, the ubiquitous Web delivered big time. Prevarication is all of three things below and perhaps even more:

lie; equivocation; lying

We intrinsically know the meaning of all of these words but here are their quick hitter definitions from the ubiquitous Web:

lie: a statement that deviates from or perverts the truth
equivocation: intentionally vague or ambiguous
lying: the deliberate act of deviating from the truth

You're wondering where the jobs are. Are you not? Even in 2017, the question persists. There are none. Moreover, Obama did not want you to have one. He was not going to solve the problem. He was the one making it worse. He wanted you to be dependent on the state. But, now, folks, there is President Donald J. Trump.

Alan Caruba in his January 26, 2010 factsnotfantasy.com blogspot hits the nail on the head. He says:

> "If Ronald Reagan was the Great Communicator, then Barack Hussein Obama will be known as the Great Prevaricator.
> ...
> Obama is so comfortable telling lies that he no longer knows the difference between the truth, a falsehood, a promise, or a casual slander. Take, for example, his recent claim that he would rather be a great one-term President than "a mediocre two-term" one. If George W. Bush wasn't around to blame for his own incompetence, Obama would have had to invent him."

Around the Web the rumblings indicate that Obama's lies have gotten so egregious that even liberals are holding their hands up and asking "what the...?"

Jack Cafferty seems to hate conservatives. So, nobody expected Jack Cafferty to be throwing his best shots at Obama on any message but like many liberals who are not on the very hard left, Cafferty is not interested in lying and he is not interested in carrying the water for a liar. Many were very surprised at Cafferty's excoriation of Barack Hussein Obama and the ineptest Congress God has ever permitted to be assembled.

"White House and Democratic leaders will hold informal, that's another word for secret negotiations, meant to shut Republicans and the public out of the process. That's a far cry from the election, when then candidate Obama pledged to "broadcast the negotiations on C-Span so that the American people can see what the choices are."
...

"President Obama hasn't even made a token effort to keep his campaign promises of more openness and transparency in government. It was all just another lie that was told to get elected."

Thank you for the truth, Mr. Cafferty

This next note on lying is from the Minister of Propaganda from the Reich. This quote is so spooky, it gives me the creeps.

How would Barack Hussein Obama feel about this quote? Perhaps it already is part of his socialist mantra, and that is the spookiest thought of all.

"If you tell a lie big enough and keep repeating it, people will eventually come to believe it. The lie can be maintained only for such time as the State can shield the people from the political, economic and/or military consequences of the lie. It thus becomes vitally important for the State to use all of its powers to repress dissent, for the truth is the mortal enemy of the lie, and thus by extension, the truth is the greatest enemy of the State."

This spooky quote is from Joseph Goebbels, a man who committed suicide along with his wife, the Fuhrer, and his wife, Eva Braun -- all together.

Why this book?—Jobs! Jobs! Jobs!

For whom did I write this book? How about for every person out there who has ever heard a government official tell them that illegal aliens do not take American jobs? How about for every person who has seen their own job go to a foreign national?

How about for every great worker out there who sees reality and reports on it and then gets slammed against the wall because their comments are not politically correct and they lose their jobs? How about for those who simply lost their jobs because their companies had to cut back because of our former president's lousy economy.

When there are very few jobs like today, companies and institutions have the upper hand. Those on the Nationalist, Populist, Conservative side of the election issues knew intrinsically that Hillary Clinton would continue to assure there were no jobs in the future but there would be lots of potentially dangerous refugees and illegal foreign nationals to take whatever jobs might come available.

It is counter-intuitive to believe that government can't create real jobs. Only the private sector can. But, government can either make it easy for the private sector to create jobs or it can make it exceedingly difficult. Our government has chosen to do the latter.

Our country and all others need a certain number of government employees to function. But, if we go back to the Employment Act of 1946, we would find that a different notion of the value of government employment has emerged. The new thinking is that government by itself can minimize downturns in economic activity by spending, "investing—the new cutesy term" in projects designed to stimulate employment. But, government has no money but what the people provide.

The government in these cases may be either a direct employer, such as when it hires more soldiers for our armed forces, or it can be an indirect employer (as when it increases by spending huge sums with contractors to build / repair federal highways.

The latter would increase employment in construction companies. It may be true that we need larger armies or better highways, but that is not how we stimulate the economy as the money comes from the people.

There is this insidious idea that still persists in socialist circles that government job creation actually generates an increase in employment. Think about the effect of construction companies adding 100,000 jobs due to a $3 billion government spending program. It cannot be argued that employment is 100,000 ahead of where it would otherwise be.

But, it just does not work because it cannot be sustained. Government merely shifts fund from one source to another. It never creates funds. Conventional wisdom would us all believe government "investments" in people create unemployment rate decreases. Yet the opposite is the case.

How is this? History proves it out. For the same years, there has been a positive, though statistically insignificant, correlation between government employment (as a percentage of total employment) and the unemployment rate. This suggests that as government work is created more jobs are lost elsewhere resulting in a rising unemployment rate. So, now that we have done away with the idiocy of that theory, where do we get jobs that are real that increase the total number of employees. But, let's digress again first

Jobs are no longer available in America because the government has stopped caring about America and Americans. The solution is not to train government to think more highly of Americans. Their job is to represent us even if they do not like us. The solution is easier than can be imagined.

When government does not do its job or it hurts the people, Americans must replace those who have sold us out. We need to elect real Americans who want to make America great again. Isn't it great that we have Donald Trump as our new president?

We had tried to get the job done by flushing out a Democratic Congress and US Senate with a Republican version. But the Republicans played us for fools and joined the Democrats. They had their own agendas and disappointed us deeply. Now, we have replaced the President but there are still too many elites in office to make President Trump's agenda, which is the people's agenda, move swiftly.

We must completely back America in two years and four years. Senators and Congressmen against America need to be removed. We know America will be great again because Donald J. Trump is President and he will not stand for it. If and when the Congress misbehaves against the people, our new President will call them out, identify them, go around them to correct the problem quickly, and have them identified for removal the next election.

Donald Trump knows how to create jobs in America by making it easy for the private sector to create jobs. They will not be government jobs. That is how we create jobs—not with government programs that uses taxes or treasury funds.

My accountant years ago, a gentleman named Jimmy Slamon explained to me while I was with IBM, about the best hedge against inflation. With a twinkle in his eye, Slamon said: "Have a job!" This whole book is about jobs. Until I lost my job as a Chief Technology Officer and in 1998 and as a university professor in 2011, and collected unemployment for the first time in my life into 2012, I always had always had a job as that valuable hedge v inflation.

Like many of you reading this book, I learned that jobs are not a given and in the eight years of Obama, good jobs have become even more scarce. Regardless of what happens to me in the future, the message in this book continues to be Jobs! Jobs! Jobs! The Donald Trump Way! With the right techniques as noted in the book titled Jobs! Jobs! Jobs!, we can bring jobs home and increase employment.

When we look back at the Congress of these United States during the Obama Administration, they simply did not do their jobs. Issue after issue from bailouts to the big porkulus bill to the huge energy tax proposed but defeated, and then the preoccupation with making the US health system into another Post Office, looking at all of this and more, a Congress working for the people was MIA.

Time to get back to work

Over the years, I found that the Congress has been voting for things that you and I know are wrong. As politicians, unfortunately, they have been doing so for an awful long time. Along with a former president who could organize a community but not a checkbook, they now have succeeded in making the economy so messed up that it will take years to recover. Along the way, the people of the US need Jobs! Jobs! Jobs! We need to be able to get back to work ASAP.

All the while that this "reshaping" of the US has been going on, through 2016, eight years after Obama was sworn in, Congress, the corrupt media, and President Obama pretended that the country was already at work. They liked to call the eight years' normal post-recession times, and they never missed an opportunity to blame Bush for the misery! It wasn't Bush at all.

It was Obama, who knew nothing about business. We are still not back to work and these are not normal post-recession times. Blame Obama but credit Trump each time he does something to make it better. Do not believe the dishonest, corrupt, biased press.

The Democrats spent all their time in office concentrating on their socialist agenda and amassing more power and hiring more government employees, rather than helping Americans get back to work. Republicans wimps merely wanted to get along with the Democrats. Only once formally, that I can recall did the President say that Jobs were the most important item on his agenda. He quickly forgot. Obama cared nothing about US jobs for US citizens.

State of the Union 2010

President Barack Hussein Obama delivered the 2010 State of the Union Address on January 27, 2010, to a joint session of Congress. It was the President's second time before a joint session of Congress. His first was a month after taking office in 2009.

The President delivered the speech on the floor of the United States House of Representatives in the United States Capitol and it was aired on all major networks. Most Americans, in fear over the economic recession, anticipated that the President would offer a solution to our woes and hopefully, it would be workable, and hopefully, he would not be kidding about it.

On cue the president touched on two of the hot topics on everybody's mind. During the speech, Obama covered major proposals for Job creation and federal deficit reduction. A fly on the wall would have thought that finally the country was going to hear about a solution that would mean Jobs! Jobs! Jobs!

Looking at the President's speech, under the category of Job creation there were three major points as follows:

1. Building clean energy facilities
2. Giving rebates to Americans who make their homes more energy-efficient
3. Slash tax breaks for companies that send jobs overseas (giving those breaks to companies that create Jobs in the U.S.)

The first two items were about energy and the third was about the President being annoyed that some American corporations were not repatriating their earnings in foreign countries. In other words, the US was not getting the tax revenue. So, the only apparently meaningful thing in the president's speech on Jobs was actually about something else. Obama never cared about jobs. It's the only answer as to why!

The next point in his speech on "Jobs" was to "encourage American innovation." On the surface one could see how this could help the Jobs situation. The funny thing about the comment is that Americans have always been innovative. Look at the list of inventors and inventions of Americans from electricity to the iPad. In the write-up of the State of the Union, as a clarifying point the part about encouraging American innovation had a subtle subtitle (focus on clean energy).

Michael Moore, the well-known progressive filmmaker and liberal thinker loves using a basketball analogy to describe President Obama. Moore says that many times President Obama "fakes right and goes left." In other words, this artful speaker is often all words and no action or different action.

Once he had convinced the folks that he was doing one thing, they relaxed and then right before their eyes he would pull the fake and go left. He would almost always if not always get away with it because nobody would expect him to be so obviously deceitful.

Obama was the master of the unexpected. For example, most of us expected him to want to be a good president. For thinking men and women, after eight years, our opinion on him wanting anything good for America and Americans has changed. He never even rooted for us.

During the 2010 State of the Union, it was the beginning of another presidential head fake. It turns out that there were few bullets of substance on jobs— mostly just lip service. His Jobs message was an energy message as the President at the time was quite desirous of having the Senate pass the Jobs killing Cap and Trade bill that had already passed the House. It is hard to be for Cap and Trade and increased Jobs! at the same time but Obama still thinks he is ambidextrous.

His second head fake was when he offered these two bones to Congress. Note again these are energy issues, not Jobs issues:

- ✓ Building nuclear power plants
- ✓ Exploring off-shore areas for oil and gas

Nonetheless, he never did either of these. If the President was interested in building nuclear power plants or exploring off-shore areas for oil and gas, we would have been doing this for the last eight years. But remember, he faked right and went left. Sorry folks, but on the Jobs thing, he was just kidding. Before we go back to the 2010 State of the Union, the defining speech of the Obama presidency, let's just see how well Mr. Obama has done on jobs.

Jobs! Jobs! Jobs! from inauguration to 2016

The President could not have liked Investor's Business Daily's report on jobs from March 2016. It brings us right up to date on success with Jobs so let's go over it now. I suspect there was too much truth in this analysis for Obama's tastes.

> For example, the President has been bragging about a 14.4 million job growth number. That sounds impressive, doesn't it? But the president's number is stretched over almost six full years, while other factors were changing concurrently. For example, during the same period, the working age population grew by 15.8 million. So, the normal growth to sustain jobs was not met. We were short by 1.4 million jobs. We have definitely lost ground on jobs under Obama.

> Besides that, the supposed 14.4 million increase in jobs is measured against when the job market hit rock bottom in February 2010 after over a year of Obama, a big recession, and no prospects for an improved economy. If you compare the current number of jobs to the previous jobs peak two-years earlier during the Bush years, in January 2008—which, by the way is how job growth is normally measured—the number of private-sector jobs has increased by just 5.6 million.

> Additionally, when we include the period from 2008 instead of beginning at 2010, during the same time, the population grew by more than 20 million. In other words, there's what can be called a "jobs gap" of more than 14 million. That is a lot of jobs that Obama policies kept out of America.

Let's now look at the figure that the President does not want any of us to see. What about "labor force participation"? This is a measure of how many people are working or activity looking for a job. Admittedly, it has recently ticked upward, it is still way below where it was when the jobs recession ended in early 2010.

Let's put this in context with the Reagan recovery. If we compare the Administration's numbers to what happened during the Reagan recovery, when the job market exploded after bottoming out in December 1982. While the population grew 12.4 million in the following six years, the number of jobs shot up by 18.4 million. Yes, I said "UP!"

As a result, the labor force participation rate—which actually started out lower under Reagan than Obama since Reagan had to overcome the stagflation of the Carter years before the engine could start-up again—zoomed upward as strong growth pulled people back into the job market. Reagan had his eyes on jobs. Obama had his eyes on ideology.

There is even more context that Obama never discusses when he brags about his "great" numbers. We already established that 14.4 million jobs were created from February 2010 to March 2016. But, this is not so good when we look at the number of people who dropped out of the labor force -- either because they retired or just quit looking for work. The number of people who for one reason or another, were no longer collecting and could no longer find a job shot up by an astonishing 10 million.

Obama's record is one he should hide because there is still more. The number of people who aren't in the labor force but do want to work is substantially higher today than when Obama took office. And the median length of

unemployment is now 11.4 weeks, which is also higher than
when Obama took office.

Investors' Business Daily offers their conclusion: "In many
areas of life, slow and steady will win the race. But when it
comes to job growth, slow and steady ends up leaving
millions of workers in the dust."

When we add to all this the fact that the jobs created were not
replacement jobs for manufacturing or meatpacking or
Information technology, they were bartenders, waitresses,
chambermaids, etc. we know that the income per job is
substantially less.

Add again to this the desire for small companies to keep their
workforces down so they would not get killed by Obamacare
expenses, and so they would not hire their 50th employee. On
top of this, those companies that need more hours from more
people who do not want anything to do with Obamacare simply
create 29-hour per week jobs.

All of this adds to the fact that Americans were suffering and
Obama had offered nothing for eight years. There are no jobs
today. Period. Of course, we do have those created by Mr.
Trump before he became President.

2010 State of the Union—more "promises"

When the President got more into the Cap and Trade energy
issues, he asked for more "investment" in advanced biofuels and
clean coal technologies. Whether the President knows it or not,
he sure does not acknowledge that American power is
dependent on coal. Coal powers most of American electricity.

That means that many jobs are dependent on coal. It is not clean
coal at this point. So this has nothing to do with solving today's
Jobs problem. Biofuels are a real joke as it takes substantial

energy to produce these fuels. Americans must keep their eye on the ball watching for the head fakes.

The President gave another head fake. The fact is that his focus on clean coal had nothing to do with getting more energy or getting more Jobs. The focus was on the carbon dioxide that is produced from burning coal due to its impact on global warming. There goes that head fake again. He was not talking about energy or Jobs. Obama was talking about global warming.

What could we believe? Not much folks! We have been victims of institutional lying from the highest levels of government on down. Yet there are still many who still do not see it These are called low-information voters. There are so many of them, you would be surprised.

Call it a head fake if you like. Say, he just faked right and then went left if you like, but in Pennsylvania we have a name for that. It is called a lie. People who do things like that are not called head fakers, they are called liars, plain and simple. Yes, Obama was kidding about Jobs and from January through March, when Obamacare passed onto 2016, that was the last of his Jobs messages. He had more important things on his mind.

Clean coal was just another head fake

At some point, even president Obama stopped talking about clean coal, which right now is a myth perpetrated by those who think they can con the environmentalists into seeing something that is not. A year or so after Obama's 2010 SOU, on July 14, 2011, American Electric Power announced it would table plans to build a carbon capture and sequestration project at its Mountaineer Plant in West Virginia. This ended the short-term notion of clean coal for West Virginia.

Yet, coal is really big in West Virginia. And, so, West Virginia University keeps looking for new ways of doing things that can make the technology even cleaner. But nothing in technology happens overnight. It takes a lot of research, and sometimes an idea takes 20 years to develop.

"If coal is going to be here for 250 years, we're going to need newer technologies as we go into the next 250 years that would make coal more energy efficient and make it easier for us to extract these technologies in a cleaner way with less damage to the environment," said Richard Bajura, director of the National Research Center for Coal and Energy at West Virginia University. That day is not here yet but recreational basketball and head fakes to the people are a real thing for sure.

Coal is extremely energy rich and it would be good if a little soap could clean it up. A single fist-size lump of bituminous coal contains about 12,000 Btu--enough energy to power a 75-watt bulb for two days. Coal is relatively easy to dig out of the ground and it is still dirt-cheap. Coal costs about 1/6 of oil or natural gas per Btu. Like it or not, a substantial portion of the industrial world was built with coal power and coal keeps it going.

Of course, coal has issues. Its ashes are not very pleasant nor is its smoke. We might call these sooty particulates. Coal also has sulfur and nitrogen compounds. These cause acid rain. And, yes, there are traces of mercury and other toxic metals in a wad of coal.

Despite the challenges of purely clean coal, coal-fired power plants are much cleaner than they once were. They are still considered bad news for the environment and human health. Despite this, it is a sure thing that in the northeast especially for many years before the natural gas revolution in the late 1960's, there would have been hundreds of thousands of deaths if there were no coal to heat homes.

The question then was can death by freezing during an excessively cold and dank winter evening be a better deal than expiring from an abundance of sooty particulates over a minimally shortened lifetime.

By the way, there is no such thing as an average lifetime. My grand mom and grand pop lived well into their eighties. Gene Wilder, one of my favorite actors died in the summer 2016 at 83. Gram and gramps lived in our home until they died. We had a Heatrola Coal Stove in between the Dining Room and the Parlor and there was a Wilkes-Barre Coal Stove in the kitchen to heat that area, cook, and provide hot water for the house. We had no coal furnace.

We took the ashes out and dumped them in the back yard in an area where grass refused to grow. Chicken or Egg? I would bet that my grandma and grandpa would say if asked that coal lengthened their lives. It is a matter of perspective. It kept them warm. It kept us all warm. It gave my uncles jobs.

The environmentalists would rather people freeze to death than have any emissions at all. It is no coincidence that many leading environmentalists are also major population control proponents. Any motivation that elevates a certain chemical composition of the atmosphere above human life is misguided at best. So, a few frozen bodies every now and then is preferable to some environmentalists than a disfigured tree a bit too close to a nearby coal chimney.

This (jobs! Jobs! Jobs!) is not a moral or immoral book though some might argue that no jobs when there can be jobs is a moral issue. Few Americans that I know would carry it as far as major elites in our society such as CNN Founder Ted Turner's perception of how to make sure the environment is clean and safe for him: " "A total population of 250-300 million people, a 95% decline from present levels, would be ideal." Why guys like Turner are not interested in more coal deaths is a mystery indeed.

A recent study concluded that coal emissions contribute to 10,000 premature deaths in the United States each year. I'd like to see that study. How do they know? Besides early deaths, they say that coal is by far the largest single source of greenhouse gases in the U.S. So, it is no surprise that coal has long been the primary target of proposals to cut air pollution and carbon-dioxide emissions. One might ask with all the emissions going on in the world, especially China, how is it that anybody or anything is alive?

Just in time to skirt the various plans to cap or tax CO2, coal is getting rebranded. In my opinion, this is claptrap. The new buzzword we already discussed is "clean coal." It is a high-tech, low-emissions fuel of the future. I don't doubt coal can be made cleaner and it should but it will never be clean and clean coal is certainly not an option today. If it were, the US would become the "Saudi Arabia of clean coal overnight." By the way, we are already listed as having more gas and oil than Saudi Arabia or any other country.

One might ask: Why try to reduce our dependence on coal today when fabulous, guilt-free clean coal is just around the corner? The facts again speak loudly: Coal will never be clean. It is possible to make coal emissions cleaner and as noted previously, we should go as far as economically possible to do so.

But coal as an energy source has helped my family live our lives in a warm home. It also has provided many jobs to many family members and others in Pennsylvania and other states. It sure can be called a poor man's fuel but it is a powerful energy source for our country.

Let's be clear. We should continue research into making coal cleaner--that fuel will be a vital part of our energy mix for decades. Right now, it is just a good thought for the future. Meanwhile we have a lot of work to do to create real-world energy alternatives that work today. All of this work and the energy we get adds to the number of jobs available and that is a good thing.

Obama, the "Jobs Man" made just a few comebacks in eight years

On January 27, 2010, we finally got the "I am the Jobs Man Message." The news of the big nothing Jobs plan did not even have a chance to hit the next day talk shows when Nancy Pelosi could contain herself no longer. Most people had not yet gotten the Obama jobs message when, bursting with self-pride, the Madame Speaker at the time purposely puppetted an overly prepared parody of herself and Obamacare to the American people. I love alliteration.

Having listened to the State of the Union and its mention of Jobs, I originally thought that the Speaker was off message. Maybe she had not gotten the Jobs message that Obama was putting forth. Nope! She knew that it was just a head fake. She read it better than any of us. Her wait was over.

She could have rolled with it a few more days so it looked more legitimate--like it was real, but I repeat, she could not contain herself. The President had to get that darn State of the Union out of the way so he could give the head fake.

Nancy Pelosi was full of glee. She caught the fake and she no longer had to wait to deliver her message, which I have word for word just below: I did add a small preamble to the Pelosi speech so it reads like the way I just described.   Here it is

[Despite what president Obama said last night, that was January 27 and that day is gone. Today is January 28 and this is a new day.]

"We will go through the gate. If the gate is closed, we will go over the fence. If the fence is too high, we will pole vault in. If that doesn't work, we will parachute in. But we are going to get health care reform passed..."

She did not mention Jobs! Nor did she intend to mention Jobs! And, nobody on the Democratic side of Congress gave her a slight poke in the shoulder to say, "Hey, what about the Jobs?" Jobs was not and still is not on the Democrat's to-do-list. After that day, Obama, the Jobs Man, went away and brought to us Obama the Obamacare Guy!

This is the nonsense that is killing our country and killing Jobs throughout the country

I thought about how I could help this poor situation on jobs. I've got a ton of various jobs solutions and they are scattered through this book and my recently revised book called RRRRRR, discussed in the prior chapter, has a ton more. President Donald Trump knows how to create jobs and they are coming bit by bit for now but soon, we will see a splurge.

One way you don't create jobs is to pass a $3 trillion health bill in the middle of a recession. That was a real jobs killer and American Corporations have been in the process of adjusting and thinning their ranks since then—specifically because of the jobs killing legislation such as Obamacare and the tons of regulations put out by this administration.

Where has Congress been on Jobs?

Why is it that the past four Congresses have not been interested in creating more Jobs for workers? Congress has not even had enough time for persuasive rhetoric. They are simply MIA while letting President Obama have his way on whatever he wants. Mr. Obama had no desire to create new jobs unless they were government jobs which do not help.

Why is it that Congress wants to give all the earnings of the working-person to the non-worker? There are two answers. Philosophically many Democrats have become socialists and more and more on the hard left espouse Marxism and Communism. Notice that after all Obama's head fakes, he goes left! Democrats see this as their calling.

Their goal is not to create more Jobs but to create more people looking for Jobs who will be dependent on government. The President is right in tune and the Republicans have overdosed on Ambien. Hopefully Congress will be as good to President Trump on Jobs!

Democrats use whatever way possible to make more Americans dependent on the hand of the government. Until Trump, they were succeeding. When you are fortunate enough to be employed, their goals affect you differently.

They want to redistribute your wages to the guy down the street who sleeps all day. They also want to buy votes with your money by giving it to somebody else. This is not our parents' Democratic Party but it nonetheless is the Party as it exists today.

Healthcare Redistribution

Democrats have this notion that if you have something that somebody else would like to have that you are selfish for keeping it. So, their programs—Obama's and Hillary's programs are to take away what you have and give it to somebody else with the authority of government agencies such as the IRS.

It is no wonder that they also believe in healthcare redistribution and though nobody talks about it like this. Democrats in Congress do not want your employer to give you healthcare benefits. They know that people who are employed typically have health insurance. Often the health policies are good. They want the people who do not work to have the same health insurance policies as you do. They want the people who never put a dime into Medicare to have the same health benefits as retired seniors.

The only way for Congress and Obama to do that is to redistribute your healthcare. Since your employer is not going to pay for people who do not work for the company, and Medicare right now, will not pay for those who are not entitled to Medicare; the solution is to take half of the value of your plan and give it to somebody else. They have been doing it for most of the Obama years.

Additionally, they have taken 1/2 of Medicare (this is in the operative bill) and given it to somebody else. This is called healthcare redistribution and it means that those who earned their health insurance are being forced through taxation and insurance rates to give it up for weakened insurance policies so that in the end, all policies are the same and there is equality.

Under the program, we find that there is less and less healthcare but there is more equality. Few people today have a good health insurance policy for a reasonable price. But there are now others who get subsidies so they can afford better policies than you. Is this why you sent your Congress person to represent you?

Rationing, longer lines in the doctor's office and the ER as well as reduced care are the natural effects. It was a bad bill and it has been hurting a lot of people who wake up and find themselves on the outside looking in. Employers are so afraid of it, they try to reduce employee hours or reduce their workforce.

The next step towards honesty is to actually call the program "healthcare rationing." At a $trillion dollars in cost, the money is coming out of somebody's pocket. It is your pocket. Moreover, $500 billion came from reduced Medicare benefits. Additionally, as we learned from the recent insurance company exodus from Obamacare, it has already cost the insurance industry many, many billions of dollars. But, they have a choice and they are bailing!

All of these socialist programs together have been slowly bankrupting this country and destroying the prospects of jobs coming back. We cannot sustain the debt. If you spent like the government, you could not even get a credit card let alone a car loan. The Chinese hold a substantial part of our debt. In other words, the Chinese own a big hunk of America -- stuff that you think you own.

When the debt gets so high that the Chinese come collecting, get ready to speak Chinese as your primary language. Maybe they will give you a Job! And, by the way, at that point, our immigration problem is solved. I can assure you, with the Chinese in charge of America, replacing Obama's Czars with commissars, English and Spanish will both be second languages.

Does it not go without saying that to make sure this new Congress with Donald Trump as President does not behave like the Republican Elite Establishment. We have Donald J. Trump as President of the United States. He is one of the only people in the world who will watch Congress like a hawk and make sure they represent the people and not their own selfish interests

Chapter 8 101 Secrets How To Be A High Information Voter

Please do not be a low information voter

Instead of your worrying about being a low-information voter, this book (101 Secrets How To Be A High Information Voter – available on Amazon & Kindle, helps you take all the worry away. By following the prescription and the 101 learning secrets, you can make the transition from low, low-medium, medium, or medium-high Information voter to high information voter. This book helps you set the path and then all you need to do is follow it.

Things are so complex in America today that many citizens who vote are not familiar with the major issues they are deciding when they make that long trip to the voting booth. This book helps change all that.

You will find references and hard facts about how to acquire the knowledge necessary to make it so obvious that you are tuned in to current events that even your friends will comment. They will be quick to notice your new abilities to dissect the facts as only high information voters can.

Your family will be impressed. Your friends will be impressed, and more importantly you will be impressed with all you know. You don't have to take college courses or sweat in libraries for days at a time. All you need is your TV and your radio. If you have a smart phone that will help as will a PC. But you can become a high information voter even without buying one thing.

It is so simple that the most important ingredient is that you want to become a high information voter! And that is that!

Never again will you be subjected to things that you do not understand. Just because one or two powerful people choose to ignore our rights and freedoms does not mean we must endure the tyranny. The first step of course is to understand the most basic written precepts. This book gets you started with 101 great ideas for success. You can't miss getting to the top of the high information class.

Introduction to Being a High Information Voter

Do you remember this? "There are eight million stories in the naked city. This has been one of them." Well, we are at the beginning of one of those stories. Many who are now reading this story never believed they would need it. Thankfully, there are not eight million secrets in this book. You need lots less than 8 million.

However, there are 101 secrets to becoming a high information voter in this book, and this introduction begins the process of bringing you the secrets. It does sets up all the other secrets. It tells you what you gain by trudging along, one secret at a time, until you have all the secrets.

Then, once the listed secrets are well known, it is time for you to get to work. You will be able to plan your learning work, and then work your learning plan. The secrets in this book will assure that you will never again be a low-information voter.

The objective is for you to never slip into the mire of the low-information voter. The only game low information voters can play is the game of blindly repeating the thoughts of others. High information voters think for themselves.

What is a low-information voter? Let's read a little bit from the guy who coined the term and then we will all know: We'll use an article by Colbert King to get us on our way. Here goes:

Introduction to Being a High Information Voter

Do you remember this? "There are eight million stories in the naked city. This has been one of them." Well, we are at the beginning of one of those stories. Many who are now reading this story never believed they would need it. Thankfully, there are not eight million secrets in this book.

However, there are 101 secrets to becoming a high information voter in this book, and this introduction begins the process of bringing you the secrets. It does sets up all the other secrets. It tells you what you gain by trudging along, one secret at a time, until you have all the secrets.

Then, once the listed secrets are well known, it is time for you to get to work. You will be able to plan your learning work, and then work your learning plan. The secrets in this book will assure that you will never again be a low-information voter.

The objective is for you to never slip into the mire of the low-information voter. The only game low information voters can play is the game of blindly repeating the thoughts of others. High information voters think for themselves.

What is a low-information voter? Let's read a little bit from the guy who coined the term and then we will all know: We'll use an article by Colbert King to get us on our way. Here goes:

Colbert King's Low-Information Definition of the Term "Low-Information Voter"

March 25, 2013

On March 25, 2013, Rush Limbaugh, trying to figure out why liberal progressives do not blame Obama for all the problems he truly has caused our country, created a new buzz-word – low information voter. In many ways the term is self-explanatory.

Here is some of what Rush said when reflecting on the Colbert King definition:

BEGIN TRANSCRIPT

RUSH: Over on PBS on their Sunday morning Inside Washington show, they had Washington Post columnist Colbert King, known to his friends in the DC establishment as Colby.

They were having a discussion about the Republican Party. Nina Totenberg said, "When you look actually at what the Republican Party analysis of itself was --"this Reince Priebus thing,"-- the fear was that the electorate is a different electorate. And it isn't just much more of a minority electorate. It is an electorate that wants some serious social and economic safety net that is different from what they are hearing from Republicans today." And this is what Colbert King had to say.

KING: The guru of the Republican Party, the face of conservatism is Rush Limbaugh. We all agree to that. He puts down those results by saying Obama won with a low-information voters, low-information voters. What's he mean by that? They're sort of stupid. They don't understand the issues.

RUSH: No, that's not... nobody in the media, I don't know what is so hard about getting me right. I'm on 15 hours a week. You don't need a password to listen to this program. It's free over the air. You can even listen to parts of this program at RushLimbaugh.com. You do not have to be a subscriber. You can access the text of this program at RushLimbaugh.com. It's free. It's everywhere. What is so hard to understand about what I say?

I have never said that low-information voters are stupid. I just said they don't know what they think they know. They are prisoners to the media, which has dumbed them down. Low-information voters can be doctors. Low-information voters can be scientists. They can be among all walks of life. It has nothing to do with IQ.

It has to do with what they don't know because of their media sources. Low-information voters are clearly people that don't have all the information available to make a voting choice. That's all they are. And they're all over the place. And most of them do vote Democrat.

Most of them did vote for Obama. It's not a comment on their intelligence. It's not that they're stupid or don't understand the issues. They just haven't had it all explained to them. What Mr. King just did here is prove himself to be a low-information columnist. He's probably a low-information voter himself. He probably closes off half of his mind to conservatism or anything else that he doesn't agree with. Just amazing.

BREAK TRANSCRIPT

RUSH: By the way, Colbert King of Washington Post, I just wanted to remind you that the term "low-information voter," I'm pretty sure that we coined it. I'm pretty sure that we made up that name, but we're not the only ones to use it. Richard Stengel, the TIME Magazine editor, was explaining why Obama was named Person of the Year. Mr. King, do you remember what Mr. Stengel said? He went on TV and he also had a press release.

They named Obama the Person of the Year because no-information voters loved the guy, and it's no-information people -- low-information voters -- who he said are transforming America. It's remarkable!

TIME Magazine said it. Obama is the guy that ended up being able to tap that block. He's the first politician to get votes from people who don't care about anything and who aren't paying attention, and that was worth honoring the president as Person of the Year. TIME Magazine, Mr. King.

END TRANSCRIPT

I do not think I need to go into my own explanation of a low-information voter. It is who none of us want to be. Limbaugh came up with the theory and he said it very well. If we choose to not follow political activity as it pertains to our country's elections and we vote in the elections without having gained the requisite knowledge to understand the orange from the green or the earth from the sky, we are doing wrong.

We would be the definition of the low-information voter. I truly believe in those circumstances, we should disqualify ourselves as voters so we do not mess up elections and put the wrong people in office.

If our minds have been molded by some pundit who we like and we never agree or disagree but merely follow, then we are basically removing our ability to make an informed choice for America. More than ever, Americans must be high information voters. Our country is at stake.

In our parents' generation, ideological candidates were not trying to undermine the Constitution and the fundamentals of our country. Today, paying attention really matters if you want to assure good leadership. President Trump is a diamond in the rough. Just think how hard it was for regular Americans to find a great leader like him.

We cannot go on with the same approach for ISIS, illegal immigration, no jobs, no respect for police and law and order, and unconstitutional actions by our country's chief executive without chipping away at our freedoms. We could not have afforded a corrupt Hillary Clinton Presidency in which she would sell parts of America to the highest bidder for Clinton Cash.

We knew that we needed someone who was not from the Democrat elite or the Republican elite. We needed a very smart man—a non-politician. We needed Donald Trump for President of the United States. {And, we got him, Praise the Lord]

I thank you all for coming here for the Information Voters 101 seminar that can be another name for this book. These are the sources for good and bad information. Choose carefully and prepare yourself to be a high information voter if you are not one already.

Once you are confident you are a high information voter, either before reading or after reading this book, please use your copy of the book to share lessons with your friends and associates on the importance of voters having the best information possible.

If you want to buy copies of this book for your friends; they are very inexpensive ($6.99 hard copy and $1.88 on Kindle). What are you waiting for?

What does this small book have in store for you?

If you get to read the book, there are 101 secrets in its first 101 pages. These secrets can help you be as smart as you ever want to be about the current state of America. My bet is that the preponderance of Americans love America and that is why I do what I do.

I also know that most Americans think it is OK to let other people, who they call politicians, run the government. Americans are trusting.

Dear Americans, unless you are evaluating a Donald Trump action, please stop being so trusting. Other politicians are no longer trustworthy.

We are kidding ourselves if we think they are really interested in representing us v themselves. What if the government says you can no longer have more than one child as in China? What if the government says, we will fill all vacancies in US firms with people less than 50 years old brought in legally or illegally from other countries in which the people have learned not to demand a high wage! Is that absurd? Would your government do that? Do you even know if it would?

I suspect that is why your face is in this book right now.

Thank you. I love America too! Here are the 101 secrets. Don't be surprised that you knew them all along. This time, use them to make sure you are a high information voter from this point on! God Bless!

Now, dear friends, here are the 101 secrets. They are shown one secret per page starting below:

In this "Make America Great Again" book we, are pleased to show Secret #1 below:

Secret #1 The Rush Limbaugh Show

Listen every day to the Rush Limbaugh show on radio from 12:00 to 3:00. If you learn nothing else from this book, this one change in your daily habits can bring you the closest to achieving high information voter status in the shortest amount of time.

Chapter 9 Healthcare & Welfare Accountability: The Trump Way:

Health Information Technology (HIT) and Electronic Accountability Records (EAR) Can Make It Happen!

President Bush and President Obama both agreed that a database of health records needed to be created and stored on behalf of the people. It is a good idea. There needs to be a record of each citizen in the United States so that it will be much easier to get a full picture of a patient in any medical provider setting. This book defines the terms for these online records and discusses the entities that would like to own your health data. The big book also offers suggestions as to which entity would be the proper custodian of such vital data.

Most Americans are aware of the major battle on health insurance and healthcare "reform" as in Obamacare, which continues in the Halls of Congress and the White House today. In 2010, Obamacare became the IT in healthcare but it was poorly conceived, poorly crafted, poorly implemented, and poorly received. In fact, to quote Pepe Le Peu, it stunk out the house.

Congress, with no Republican votes, decided to spend a trillion dollars on a government take-over of healthcare to improve lives of just 17% of the people and disrupt the lives of the other 83%

by rationing their care, providing less medical provider choices, and more taxes.

You cannot take $500 billion from Medicare for Obamacare and make Medicare better. Will senior citizens have to find employment again to buy back what has been stolen by government without their permission?

The big winners of course are trial lawyers and the big insurance companies. The people are left holding the bag. In this book, we describe in reasonable detail in words that any American can understand, how to make the healthcare system -- both ER care and Medicaid-- more accountable so that Medicare does not have to pay the price for all. There is no free lunch and this book shows the technology solutions that can help you avoid having to pick up the tab

Because government healthcare solutions are a form of welfare, this book also shows how to account for the freeloaders who all of a sudden win the PowerBall.

How about a free lunch? The US government gives millions of lunches away every day. Do you get one?

When I updated this original 2008 book about then current, domestic, political and constitutional issues intertwining with public consciousness, I became immersed, once again, in that vortex of all-too-familiar concerns about our government. I was compelled to add a few paragraphs about the Obama Presidency considering the transparent failures of the coronated Administration.

As I undertook the task of updating, I became so smothered in the existential issues that had since developed that I was pushed to delve further into the examination of the underlying issues. Thus, the project moved beyond what one may consider to be a standard update/ revision to the point that, when I received the book back from the editor, I noticed that she had split the original book not once but twice and had created two additional, entirely distinct books.

An update to the first book, *Obama's Seven Deadly Sins*, was released concurrently with this book in the summer. It advises that the deadliest sin of all is indeed Obama's approach to healthcare, or what many now call Obamacare. This book, *Healthcare and Welfare Accountability: The Trump Way*, was within Obama's Seven Deadly Sins as a chapter and when split, it was first originally released as *Healthcare Accountability*.

The Editor separated it because its message was off the mark for that book. However, she noted that it offers a coherent, common sense solution to the biggest problem with US healthcare for all - - its huge cost. It happens that the same overall solution can be applied to the current costly US welfare system.

She suggested that it be released as its own separate offering and that's what I did. The original book, *Healthcare Accountability* offers a unique and compelling solution to the problem of healthcare cost. It is still available on Amazon & Kindle.

The book is based on a notion that other writers have chosen never to explore -- individual accountability. It is inherently against the socialist model of the Democrats. The additional chapters on welfare accountability blend well into the overall theme.

Most Americans are aware of the major battle regarding health insurance and healthcare "reform" that was at its peak in the fall of 2009. Both houses were ready for conference amidst a torrent of claims of sleazy deals for Senate votes. Though the people were dead against it, the Congress, ruled by Democrats, was more than ready to spend a trillion dollars or more on a government take-over of healthcare, which ultimately passed in March 2010 as Obamacare.

The purpose of the take-over was, purportedly, to improve the lives of 17% of the people -- those that the government determined to have no access to healthcare, a determination with which many constituents tend to disagree. After all, what is Medicaid?

Unfortunately, the plan was designed to disrupt the lives of the other 83%, by reducing their healthcare access and adding more taxes to their burden. Senior citizens would eventually pay the most to support this block of 17%, which despite Congress and the president's promise does include illegal aliens.

Logic dictates that you cannot take $500+ billion from Medicare to make it better. Will Senior Citizens have to find employment again to buy back what they will gave up to Obamacare?

The big winners, in this scenario, were the trial lawyers and the big insurance companies. The people (as in We the People) were left holding the bag. In this Accountability book, we describe, in reasonable detail and in words that any American can understand how to make the healthcare system -- both ER and Medicaid, and the remnants of Obamacare more accountable to the people.

It is a simple idea so that people on Medicare do not have to bear such a high price for all. There is no free lunch and this book shows the technology solutions that can help all Americans avoid having to pick up somebody else's health tab.

In order to attain accountability, we must begin to keep track of things. President Bush and President Obama both agreed that a database of citizen health records needed to be compiled and it is, indeed, a very good idea.

In such a system, there would be health records for each citizen in the United States. In this way, it would be much easier to get a full picture of a patient in any medical provider's setting. You go in, give your cards, and poof, the provider you have never met has your permanent medical record known as an Electronic Health Record.

This book provides a logical and clear blueprint that defines the terms for organization of online database records and discusses the entities that are positioned to "own" your health data. It also offers suggestions specifying which entity would be the proper custodian of such vital data.

This book (Accountability) identifies the best means of managing the collection of health records in a "system in the sky." Additionally, the book helps Americans understand the issue and gives a solution that assures privacy and locks out the bad guys who want your health data so bad they can taste it. As a bonus, it offers a cogent solution for welfare accountability.

The Electronic Account/ Accountability System

The state of all healthcare software for practice management, as well as Electronic Health Records (EHR) processing for veterans and other government-run systems, is described in these two words, hodge-podge. This patchwork of apparently good intentions can continue doing its job, where applicable, while a new system built from the top down is implemented.

The first phase of the implementation would be the design and construction of the EHR databases. This would use the best of breed existing systems design plus all of the non-implemented enhancement requests that are desirable. Additionally, room would be made for future notions that would not be online in the short-term.

Design the Databases

The second phase would be the design and construction of the EAR databases. This is the Electronic Account/ Accountability record, which in a normal business, might be called Accounts Receivable. The EAR database would be simpler than the EHR database to design and build.

In many ways it would take on the shape of a sophisticated open item accounts receivable system in which all unpaid medical bills from all approved sources would be posted as due. The database would also hold payment information and adjustments that have been applied to any particular medical bill.

Each patient (US Citizen or not) would have a total balance owed that cross-footed to the total of all the charges, adjustments, and payments. This would assure the accuracy of the system. Each time an account is updated, the cross-foot would occur, and once a day, a cross-foot would be performed on all accounts. The big difference between this accounts receivable system and any other is that the payee could be different for every billing entry.

Who would use the EAR system?

If, for example let's say we have patients from assigned risk insurance companies, and the consortium has agreed to account for these perhaps indigent medical bill payers. The scenario would include the Insurance Company having paid the hospital or the doctor for radiography service, for instance, but the patient, has chosen not to make the co-payment or, for some reason, has defaulted in their payment to the insurance company.

If this were an approved scenario, the EAR database would need to be built to store the relationship between the care provider and the insurance company that has paid some or all of the bill to the care provider. For such transactions, the EAR system would need to be designed so that it could assign the bill for check payment or electronic payment to the proper party, if it is ever collected.

I would expect that insurance companies would be happy to pay the EAR system for collecting unpaid balances and this would be a source of public treasury revenue. Quite frankly, I do not know whether I would want the EAR system to go that far, but it is conceivable and the software can be designed to be very accommodating.

Any Medicaid transaction would be posted as unpaid and the EMTALA balances, after the hospital or other provider has tried to collect them, would be posted as open and unpaid to the provider. As many know, The Emergency Medical Treatment and Labor Act (EMTALA) is a federal law that requires anyone coming to an emergency department to be stabilized and treated, regardless of their insurance status or ability to pay.

Some methods would need to be developed to determine the split between the state and the federal government but that would be a political thing, long after the technical pieces to accommodate the scenario were in place.

Patient payments would be able to be made via check or credit card or in person to any participating EAR provider for any EHR bill. Just like the banking system reconciles checks from banks all over the world, so also can an EHR type system reconcile the from / to of payments from across the US.

The objective, of course, would be for all medical providers to be participating. Small fees for collection of debt that was not theirs could be given the onsite institutions (care givers typically). Initially, a servicer should be used to handle the checks and money orders that would be mailed directly to the EAR facility and to provide "customer service."

As the volumes of transactions are better understood, the EAR enterprise would need to be staffed with enough clerical personnel to handle the processing of the checks and money orders. Third party customer service in America may be the preferred long term solution, and, inadvertently, provide plenty of American jobs on American soil!

Again, the intent of the EAR subsystem in the EHR system would not be to be an active collection agency for all providers. Its primary purpose would be to assure that any unpaid medical bill, regardless of its source, EMTALA, Medicaid, or anything else that is authorized, is associated with an individual and listed as due until the person dies or pays the bill.

There could be a small processing fee for Medicaid or for EMTALA or any government mandated act of charity for a patient, collectable only if the patient or holder of Medicaid insurance makes payments.

Hospitals and clinics and other providers that are not part of the ownership of the organization, who wish to use the power of this system to collect co-pays, or other fees, if such work were approved, could be assessed a small charge for such services for each item collected.

In addition to the practice management software, this would be another source of revenue for this new public enterprise. Obviously, the database in the sky would need to be designed to handle all of this and more.

Question from anonymous reader: Can you tell me a little more about this electronic account record. I don't see that in any of the literature of the day?

More on Electronic Accounts Receivable

The same private HIPAA compliant company that handles the EHRs would also support EARs. Each time a doctor updates an EMR system and provides the health information and services, the software can also be set to accept the billing and payment information to "the system in the sky."

The billing and payment information would update the patient's Electronic Account Record and log the amount due for any type of patient, including Medicaid patients. Emergency rooms under EMTALA would also have access to the EAR subsystem and would be able to update it with any billing data for which the patient is responsible

Once formed, the same doctors who had initially enlisted would "own" the EAR/ EHR Company. Insurance companies would be able to interact with the company under rules specified by the board, comprising of many doctors and such, as described above.

Individuals would be able to pay any company with an EAR affiliation for any of the balances they may have accrued, regardless of the source of the service.

EDI Would Make It Smooth

EDI (Electronic Data Interchange) transactions described in more detail previously, would need to be designed for providing conversational input and output to/ from the EHR/ EAR systems. Once the transaction types were designed, just as in regular business EDI systems, conversations between the EHR/ EAR system and the practice management systems used in all provider shops (Doctor's Offices, labs, etc.) could theoretically begin.

Software vendors wishing to participate would have to incorporate the new transaction types within their packages in order to participate. Therefore, the EHR/ EAR system would not force any existing software company to go out of business. Everyone would be welcome using new standard EDI formats.

Practice Management Software for Doctor's Practices

To help one or two-person doctor's offices and small clinics and to aid in getting the system live prior to all of the software vendors coming on board, I would recommend that this new enterprise also build a small, Web based medical practice management system (MPMS). This would be the preferred tool to be used in all small medical providers' offices.

I have not evaluated whether the EHR/ EAR server complex should run the MPMS system as a service, but perhaps it should. It could be built on a separate server complex to avoid the potential of one system (EHR v EAR) crashing each other, but it would be very closely related and much of the code would be similar and re-usable in both systems.

The first cut would not be built as a Cadillac system, but rather as a software package that could handle most of the options available for a Doctor's practice in a simple manner.

The fully standardized EMR/ Practice Management System Package that would be built could be licensed and then marketed on a commission basis by all the software companies that today have their own systems and who now create incompatible code. Their potential customers would be all providers, regardless of whether they are part of the EAR/ EHR ownership group or not.

Doctor's offices that are part of the ownership of the "System in the Sky", should be able to access the practice management software for a smaller fee. Software companies and others could offer support services to any provider, whether they receive practice management software access because of their PAAC affiliation or because they license it from one of these vendors.

Like all of the software that would be built to support EHR and EAR this would be HIPAA compliant. The same EHR/ EAR databases built for the big EHR/ EAR system would provide the basis for the MPMS system. Therefore, like all good Practice Management Systems it would provide the following facilities:

- Electronic patient history statements
- Electronic claims processing
- Electronic submission of medical claims.
- EOB's (posting of electronic payments)
- Scheduling appointments
- Creation of super-bills customized for each patient
- Claims tracking
- Flexible reporting facilities

Additionally, the MPMS would provide the following facilities to interface with the EHR/ EAR System:

- EHR and EAR inquiry
- EHR and EAR custom/ query reporting
- EHR and EAR automatic input
- EHR and EAR automatic payment processing.

Get a New Tire

Eventually, after patching an old bicycle tire so many times that there are patches on patches and the whole tube gives the appearance of being no more road worthy than a bubble gum tire, everybody must eventually yield to the purchase of a new tube or a new tire.

Too many little messes out there eventually create one big mess. This big mess is not going to get fixed by fixing one little mess at a time. In fact, it may get worse. So, it really is time to replace it all, but not all at once. Regardless of how good the new systems may be, the big bang theory of software implementation does not work well.

All "at once" projects are doomed to failure. The only thing that the big bang theory ever created that was usable was mother Earth, and even that is questionable. At the time of the hypothetical big bang, this earth had no people on it; so, the big bang in many ways was a reset to zero with no systems active. No people observed and recorded this phenomenon.

The big bang theory would not work if government took over all health insurance immediately and it won't work if we pull the plug on all other software when we get the EHR/ EAR system and the MPMS systems up and running. The ticket to success is incremental implementation.

The design of the end objective databases to hold health records, as well as patient account records, accommodates the highest level of software function that could be achieved by any medical practice management system (MPMS).

The EDI transaction definitions and native support in the EHR/ EAR system would permit any and all software to be able to interface with this new high level facility. In other words, without touching the guts and basic logic of any practice management software system out there, by adding a few EDI transaction- types to the mix, the dream of EHR and the benefits of EAR can be achieved with substantial conferencing. Though none of it may be done licketty-split, it would not be a forever undertaking either.

Moreover, as an added benefit, small practices that choose to use the simple MPMS system would immediately have EMRs, EHRs, and EARs at their fingertips. Additionally, the new consortia enterprise of mostly Doctors and high level medical providers could make a small amount of revenue by renting the MPMS software access to the small practitioners at a phenomenally low price and to others as needed at going market prices. The government if honest, could help in this endeavor.

The new enterprise supporting the EHR and the EAR could actually make the physicians and small clinics an offer that their business sense can't refuse, and we, the patients, would all benefit.

Additional Proof that the System is Workable

Cash transactions at an ATM, or checks electronically sent among banks, use a similar notion to EDI called the Automated Clearing House (ACH) and a protocol called the Electronic Funds Transfer System or EFTS.

Financial institutions not only send information using EFTS, but through the central ACH, they can distribute real cash transactions among many banks or financial institutions who are members of the Automated Clearing House.

In many ways, our American banking system is based on EFTS working flawlessly with EDI as the underlying transaction formatting protocol.

You benefit also when you receive a check, such as your paycheck or SS check via EFTS. Yes, Senior Citizens get their social security checks directly deposited using the ACF and EFTS. EFTS is so similar to EDI that over time the names were merged and it is now known as EFTS/ EDI.

Why is this important? The fact is that the underlying systems to support electronic messages and electronic funds transfer are already in place. It may be that an existing EDI format might be able to be used to accommodate the EAR system for input and acknowledgments. I suspect some creative design is also necessary.

If not, the base EDI transactions can be modified to support the function and be made to take advantage of the existing infrastructure for provider to EAR/ Clearinghouse communication.

Hospitals and clinics probably would have no problem communicating to the EAR clearinghouse, but private doctors may very well have initial issues. That's why we recommend the building of the MPMS system by the Consortium.

To handle billing transactions and payment transactions and even adjustment transactions, EDI forms can be modified, or built from scratch, permitting small doctors' offices to participate in one of the most exciting undertakings ever implemented.

Let's hope Congress does something like this rather than take over the whole system. Let's make sure we undo the Stimulus language that removes the public from any rights to their own medical records.

Personal Health Records (PHR)

In addition to the "System in the Sky" approach for EHRs and EARs, PHRs are vital for this system to work even more effectively. A personal health record is medical information that is in the possession of an individual patient (or patient's non-professional caregiver). Picture a memory stick or a cell phone type device that has all the storage needed for your personal health record -- a copy of the record from the "System in the Sky"! PHR is health data on a memory stick. What a great system design.

End Note

Well, ladies and gentlemen, that is about it for the healthcare accountability portion of this book (Accountability). I hope you liked it. Throughout this book, we gently coasted to crescendo. The idea is that along with (1) building an EMR and EHR system, we should (2) build an EMR/ EHR/ EAR aware practice management system for doctors to assist in their acceptance of technology, and we should (3) build an electronic account/ accountability system along with the EMR/EHR system in the sky, and all private software packages should talk to the "sky" via EDI or a better technology.

We discussed the reasons why the EHR system and the database in the sky have great value in reducing medical errors, especially those that can result in the death of the patient.

The groundbreaking material in this book has to do with accountability. In healthcare, it is called patient accountability. I have been out to several Web sites trying to see what the reaction might be to any system that asks a receiver of benefits to one day give back to the system if they ever come back from their financial crisis. I was not looking for ways to move people off the welfare rolls or deny anybody access to life saving treatment.

What I found was there are some very kind people on liberal blogs and there are some very practical and kind people on what would appear to be conservative blogs.

The kind bloggers clearly seem to believe that the government is actually an entity that has a life of its own and has its own resources. Most do not see government, as I do, which is like a club that has membership from the full population and all the members of the club provide the funding for the club.

The members are motivated to support the club because there are things that one person does not do well, such as build roads, defend all the members from harm from another club, and other acts that are done better with group power.

The charter of the club says that the purpose is to promote the common good and does not give anybody in office an ability to confiscate dollars from the club treasury to give to any particular club member, or group of club members for any purpose.

If a club member is down on their luck then the goodness of the human being would motivate club members individually, not collectively, to reach down and help those in need. That's the club I see as the government. Any confiscation of the treasury for any other purpose would not be permitted by the by-laws.

The by-laws of the club also presuppose that self-determination and individualism, not community good and group-think, are how the individual members run their lives outside of the club.

So, the notion of confiscation of club members' investment in the club for any purpose would not be expressly forbidden. If my investment of the club were to be squandered on things with which I did not agree, that were against the by-laws, then I would want to leave that club. Wouldn't you?

Yet, because most see government as something funded by the pot at the end of the rainbow and not by donations from club members, when asked if welfare people, when they are on their feet should give back to the people's treasury, on the liberal blog sites, most voted no.

It was over 90% who believed that the welfare recipient, regardless of whether they eventually became a millionaire or not, should never have to pay back the money they received and used to sustain themselves from the people who kindly donated while they were on welfare.

None of these kind people ever offered a dollar value on how much they personally were willing to contribute because, after all, it would be better for the nasty rich, whose wealth would be legally siphoned by the government, to provide this service.

Why would anybody repay the rich? Barack Obama has defined rich as $200,000 per year in salary after stumbling on a number for a long time during his campaign. Soon, there would be no rich and no middle class if it were up to BHO. But, that was not the thrust of this book.

I saw no mention (no posts, anywhere) of the idea that it might be appropriate for those, including illegal aliens and foreigners who use EMTALA or Medicaid for their health lifeline, to ever have to pay anything it back.

I suspect that is because the same kind people who believe the millionaire should keep the cash value of his or her prior government handouts sincerely believe that people have a right to healthcare and thus its value should never be paid back to the people who pay for it.

As an American, I can see freedom as well as life, liberty and the pursuit of happiness, as benefits of the Constitution. But from my eyes, once any person's rights start costing somebody else their savings, the first person's rights end and stealing begins.

In the club analogy, you would have no rights to any of the wealth of the club and other members would ask you to turn in your membership if you became a drain on their lives.

Government has no wealth other than what it confiscates from the people and our government has already borrowed about $50,000 per person more than what the club members have paid in. Should the club go under?

I go through this so that you do not think that I am hard hearted. I think that individuals have a moral obligation to help the needy, but if they choose not to, it is over. It is their choice. There should be no enforcement to the many moral obligations we have in life. If there were, churches would be the government.

It is nobody else's mission to steal from one who chooses not to help, even if it is to make sure they pay their "fair share." What's yours is yours and God forgive me if I take any of yours. What's mine is mine and God forgive you if you take any of mine.

Nobody has a real responsibility to anybody else, other than in the precepts of their religion. The state assigns no moral duty to the citizen. In the US, we have freedom of religion, but more importantly, we have freedom, period.

We would live in chaos without such simple rules of conduct. When government is in between the stealer and the loser, it sanitizes the whole process of theft of wealth and that is just as wrong as if I steal directly from you or you steal directly from me. Our personal freedoms end at the door of the person whose freedoms we may violate.

So, being the big thinker that I am, and having the database talents to teach and to consult in the area, I know that as an adjunct to the EMR /EHR system that everybody wants, it would be a substantially smaller amount of work to piggyback on the EMR/ EHR system that is already funded to be built than if this idea were standalone.

We need an EAR database. The EHR and EAR systems databases can be related so that by accomplishing one with a bit more work, the people of the US can keep track of who owes for Medicaid services and EMTALA and a host of other services that heretofore were forever uncollectible. Why is that OK?

The purpose of this book then is not to prescribe all of the ways that the EAR system can be used to help the people of the United States, but to suggest that it can help. And, because it can help, at a time when so much funding is being dedicated to the building of the EHR system as the database in the sky, this other project should be built immediately and along with the HER system.

And, of course, I would not be me if I did not caution all Americans who want to retain their freedom that the building of the Barack Obama National Patient Database is underway. If the people are not smart this may soon become the Hillary Clinton National Patient Database I don't like either of those notions one bit. Neither should you.

It is a more sinister notion than the Insurance Companies of America's National Patient Database (which actually does exist) and I am not for that either. We the People must stop the nonsense of government, as in the kind of Orwellian notions we saw in the book 1984.

Sometimes it is good to drive arguments home ad absurdum. In this light, I present to you the bumper sticker of the year for 2009. See Figure 13-1.

Figure 13-1 Bumper Sticker Found on Internet, Summer 2009

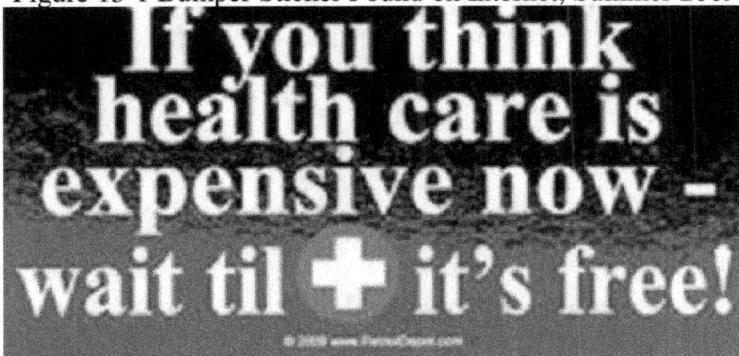

You Give Treatment; You Get Paid!

Just so you know, President Donald J. Trump believes in the safety net. Nut, he also believes in accountability. He is a good man. He believes that we should help helpless people but he also believes that government programs should not make people helpless.

Unlike many in the prior administration such as VP Biden, Donald Trump believes that he and other wealthy Americans such as Mr. Biden and Mr. Obama and Hillary Clinton should relinquish their Social Security benefits. He knows that widespread fraud exists in the Medicare, disability insurance, and food stamp programs. Trump supported the 1996 Welfare Reform Act's work requirement.

Nobody really wants to be lectured about anything. Nobody wants to be put down when they are already down. Nobody wants the safety net that they always believed was between them and the end to be weakened or destroyed. Nobody wants what is theirs to be taken away so that somebody else can have it, no matter how deserving the other may be. Most everybody believes that when you can provide for yourself, you should provide. Mostly everybody believes that anybody who chooses not to work for their own, should not be able to take theirs.

The whole idea of Healthcare Accountability, as promulgated in this book, is so that patients are comfortable asking for treatment for health problems. Everyone should be treated. Nobody suggests that anybody should ever ignore symptoms just because it would cost the state less to support if the symptoms went unaddressed. That may be the unwritten rule in Obamacare, but even Congress will not admit that.

My fear is that this new state, this highly society-oriented state, that does not care about individuals, would be quite happy if many of us would choose to die rather than collect our social security checks and spend our Medicare dollars. That is not the theme of this book, but it is the deal of the new bureaucracy in the Obamacare driven government, which I pray will end any day now. If you have a weakness that will cost Obama some cash, the subtle message is: why not just end it? Take the pipe and save the country some dough.

The bureaucrats are chomping at the bit to be freed to regulate us in ways that benefits society rather than individuals. This is the calling card of Dr. Ezekiel Emanuel who was, of course, a major Obama Health Advisor and major advocate of healthcare rationing. Emanuel is well published regarding his suggested system of healthcare rationing based on what he calls the "complete lives system."

The complete lives system "discriminates against older people" in that it values how much time a 60-year old theoretically has left on earth as a major determinant compared to say, a ten-year old. If there were a lot of ten-year old's in line, sixty-year old's would (according to Emanuel's ideas) be sent home, without the need to pack ever again.

You cannot make the stuff up that Emanuel's spews out as medical recommendations. As Obamacare's chief bioethicist, Ezekiel Emanuel, wrote that he wanted to die at 75, and he strongly implied that we should too. Everybody should have time to pick a nice casket.

Recently, he began to suggest that you could be as healthy as he is by refusing your annual Obamacare checkup. He wrote a piece for the goofy Gray Lady titled, "Skip Your Annual Physical:"

"Not having my annual physical is one small way I can help reduce health care costs — and save myself time, worry and a worthless exam. Around 45 million Americans are likely to have a routine physical this year." Emmanuel thing it is better to save the government a nickel than to save your own life. Are we not glad that goof is gone?

I happen to like the idea that healthcare, to an extent, is either unlimited or self-limiting. Those who can pay get it and those that cannot pay are at the mercy of those that can. In the EAR plan, the notion is brought forth that all patients can pay since the system automatically, in essence, writes a loan for all the patients that qualify for EMTALA care or the Medicaid insurance that a patient who cannot pay right away consumes.

I do worry about the subtleties and the coldness of an administration that is willing to permit women to die as individuals for the greater cost-saving of society. Why get that Mammogram?

Fox news Sunday addressed rationing the day after the Senate approved debate on their Obamacare bill six years ago. It was after a week in which the bureaucrats let loose with their recommendations on Mammograms and perhaps also on Pap tests. The news for those listening was that the idea of women dying had just become OK because it "costs too much" for society to find out which 40-year-olds are going to get cancer. Hmmm!

On Fox, the Segment 2 Guest was Dr. Bernadine Healy, U.S. News & World Report's Health Editor & Former Director of the National Institutes of Health (NIH). She passed away in 2011. She was an impressive person and minced no words calling this bureaucratic bumble of Obamacare rationing at its finest. She acknowledged that the bureaucrats recognize that their guidelines will mean that more women die of breast cancer but she suggests that is okay in the minds of the bureaucrats because dollars will be saved.

On the same show, the late Arlen Specter talked about "outsourcing" the downgrading of Medicare by $500 billion to assure the cuts are made as the Congress can then pull a Pontius Pilate on its implementation and blame it on the guys they hire. Get out the water basin.

I believe in individualism and that every member of society should fight as hard as they can so that every other member of society should be kept well. I do not believe healthcare is an inalienable right, but I do believe it is a duty of all to assure that no one goes without proper treatment. I do not think that the mythical collectivism of society would be enhanced while we knowingly make decisions about the type of people who are permitted to survive in the future. An initiative that would allow the bureaucrats to become grim reapers is an absolute abomination and completely avoidable.

Think of the notion of the EAR as a loan and ask yourself if this cannot expand the ability of our system to pay for healthcare. Think about the individual and the individual's three people within—me, myself, and I, as being held accountable as the number one reason why any of us get to be and to stay healthy. It is time for Healthcare Accountability.

I can't wait with Trump until Obamacare is dead because it has rationing provisions within it that have no place in society. I want no government program in its place.

With Obamacare or its replacement, there will always be the fear that one is not declared a weak member of society by some automaton bureaucrat. I had a light fear for years about being singled out by one of those "nothing-else-to-do" Obamacrats as one who does not deserve the healthcare for which I am already paying through the nose. I suspect many of you feel the same way.

Anyway, I trust that the smart people in America will read books like this and some of my others and the others will listen to people like Michael Savage and Rush Limbaugh so that we do not let the Marxists doom us to an early grave simply because we have had a cold for more than two weeks or some other blather.

Don't forget how nice it will be when everybody can contribute to their own healthcare, either while they are on their feet or off. Personal accountability should make everybody feel lots better.

.

.

One Last Anecdote

Once there was a family that had two sons. One son was very tuned in and very smart and he worked hard to make sure that the family did well. The other son was very smart but he used his smarts to be lazy and he felt like since he was born by his parents, they should make sure he was okay.

The industrious son was always told that his brother needed special care, but, deep down he knew they were equal. As the sons got older, the parents, approaching the end of their lives, began to give them both part of their savings in equal proportions.

The industrious son was never heralded for his good works. Yet, much of the parent's saving had come because of the industriousness of this son who had worked hard every day. As this son observed equal shares given to his brother who chose not to work, he was confused about what to do. So, he decided that he too would take life easy and disbursements began to exceed resources and income. Eventually, the family fell out of prosperity and ... well, maybe it did not have to end this way.

When things are not fair, very often individuals change their behavior to even up the score. If work has no payoff, why work?

We are all accountable and to ensure continued prosperity we must all be held accountable for our actions and our debts. Our nation was built on the blood, sweat and tears of a generation that equated personal accountability with the very freedom that we have enjoyed for generations henceforth. It's not too late to unite, as individuals, to fight for our own right to have a role and our own accountability in our healthcare process.

Now, I am going to show off by signing off in a way that just came to me: Gesundheit!

Chapter 10   Take the Train to Myrtle Beach—The Trump Way

OK! Amtrak does not directly serve Myrtle Beach; but it should!

Donald Trump is working hard as our new President so that among other great things, he can restart private passenger railway systems in America. The Trump Way will get you all the way to Myrtle Beach by rail with no rental cars, busses or overnight hotels required. President Donald J. Trump, the Master Builder can get the job done where others have failed.

This book tells you how to get to Myrtle Beach by train from anywhere in the Northeast today but when Mr. Trump begins to focus his attention on the railways system. It will be much easier. The full book with the title as shown in the Chapter heading above is available at Amazon.com and Kindle. It also tells you about all the top trains in the world and what needs to be done in America so we can be tops in trains and rail systems. Then, we all could get to Myrtle Beach and lots of other great places in our beautiful country by train with no sweat.

President Donald J Trump knows that government cannot run anything for too long as there is no entrepreneurial spirit in government chieftains or regular government employees. There is no real incentive to do one's best. Trump is very familiar with the Conrail story when the government was losing money on freight train hauling in the US.

The solution was to privatize it and make it the most successful cargo train system in the world. Donald Trump has his eye on the passenger railway system that is run about as good as it can be today by Amtrak; yet it keeps losing money and it still uses old slow borrowed tracks from the former Conrail system.

Consequently, often Amtrak passenger trains are stuck behind slow-moving Cargo trains when they miss a set of tracks by just a few minutes. For passengers, it can be as much as a two to three-hour delay. Americans would love to lay more track in the US. Trump would like them to have those great paying jobs. Would it not be nice if a consortia of wealth people were to get together and make high speed railway a go in the USA?

Less than ten years ago, in our own neighborhood, which had been dismantling huge railroad bridges that once hauled large amounts of freight through Pennsylvania, we heard the horn from a big diesel locomotive once again. The big diesels and big freight trains have come back and wherever they go, they are making big money for their investors.

Today, I learned that the reason the huge trains stop right by our house is not to find the last car, but they discovered a Burger

King at the bottom of a huge earthen trestle a few blocks away. The trestle bridges keep these huge freight trains from impeding the traffic flow in our area of NEPA.

A hungry lunch designee spoke to us and said that the freight was coming from Syracuse to Pittsburgh and the Burger King order would be consumed by the folks tending this huge train that seemingly never ended. He of course would be one of the many enjoying the Burger King fare.

Consequently, it made me again think about the one-time successful American Railroad Industry that ran both Passenger and Freight across the fruited plains. At one time, freight trains blocked city streets for as much as a half-hour at a time but then they went away—literally. They disappeared. The Freight by train industry is doing so well today that more and more trains are using the track that was left to expand the railroad industry in the US.

I am glad you found this book. I sure hope that you found it in time for your next great vacation. You should not have to hop a freight train to get there. You can take an Amtrak passenger train.

If you have never been to Myrtle Beach, the pleasure is all yours. Myrtle Beach is one of the most beautiful and exciting vacation spots in the United States if not the world. Train travel is definitely the most exciting and the most scenic, and the least intrusive way to go from place to place in America when the distance is not more than 1000 miles.

If you choose to ignore the 60 miles from Florence SC to Myrtle Beach at the end of your train ride, you can get there in just about nine hours from Philadelphia, all the while enjoying the ambience of what some think is a bygone era. When you hit your train destination, you will not be in Myrtle Beach, but you will be close enough. You will need to rent-a-car or bus or limo service but you will already have a smile on your face. My wife Pat and I took the trek on the train and we rented a car From Florence to get to Myrtle Beach. It sure was exciting.

In this book, you will learn that not only can you get there from here, the trip will be better than you ever thought it might be. The train ride will be spectacular. You will also see how neat it would be if there was a spoke rail line that went right to Myrtle Beach. I bet with the proper motivation from folks like you, the leg from Florence to Myrtle Beach will be first on the Trump list of rail projects. I know that I would personally love that.

On the train that ends in Florence and on most Amtrak trains, you will find club car service, mini sleepers and full bedrooms. Along the way there is even time for a cocktail or two while reading about Myrtle Beach in your AAA Guidebook. By the way, you don't have to bring your own cocktails and sneak over on the side of the road to drink them. The Bar car on the train does the job! You also get a dinner and a breakfast included in the ticket price.

When you get to Myrtle Beach, you will find that a world of natural wonderment opens for your enjoyment. I had been waiting for fifteen years to go back to Myrtle Beach to experience its clean and golden sands. As soon as I discovered, through copious research, that my beauty and I could get to Myrtle Beach by train, I asked my wife Pat, if it was OK? She almost immediately said "y-e-s." Those three little letters mean so much!

While telling you how to get to Myrtle Beach the best way via Amtrak, I was also compelled as a writer to discuss how the US train experience compares with the European and the Chinese experience. And of course, because I am a dreamer, I spend a bit of time fantasizing about what will happen when the US builds high speed rail across the country and the timing of flights and train travel become very close. Wow!

I hope you enjoy the big book titled, Take The Train to Myrtle Beach – The Trump Way, and please enjoy the snippets we show in this work. It is all about the Master Builder making America great again. A full and complete railroad infrastructure would sure help America rise to the top again. Wow!

The Trains of Europe Compared with Amtrak

In 1971 when the number of companies that made up the US Railway Industry believed they could not profitably compete in passenger service, the US government formed the Amtrak Corporation, a government owned private corporation to run passenger service across the US from coast to coast and more.

Let's check out Europe, then America!

Prior to your getting jealous of the foresight of our European brothers and sisters in bringing train technology up to date and making it desirable for all human beings, I would like to tell you that the sun is about to appear from the eight-year cloud that has been enveloping the US of A.

Not only did we not see an improvement in our passenger railway system with a Democratic President who believes in all things Democrat, but despite giving the former President just under $900 billion to reconstruct our public infrastructure which included railways and highways and bridges, he used it as a slush fund to keep union jobs during the recession. If you did not work for a union, you paid for the former President's largesse.

Most unaffiliated US citizens did not benefit. We got none of the big money—just the unions to keep their workers healthy while the rest of America was almost starving. Then after getting the money the President joked like it was funny that there were really no shovel-ready jobs. He got a big kick out of it while as a millionaire, he was living in the White House, not in every day America.

This is my second cut at this book and the essence is not much different than the first round. Most spelling errors are gone but the theme is the same—how to get to Myrtle Beach despite the government placing obstacles in your way. I did it and know how to do it again. Of course, I know a Trump Administration can upgrade the facilities and make it a better deal for all Americans to get to Myrtle Beach from anywhere.

Yes, the big difference this time is that America does not have to beg a President who may not even like Americans to do something that would help Americans. We gave him almost $900 trillion and he spent it assuring he would get reelected and he did. He bought a lot of votes with that $900 billion. Hillary Clinton had said that her administration would be just like Obama's and that may be why she has had to buy a lot of yarn and knitting needles recently.

I liked a lot of the candidates for President in 2016 especially Ted Cruz and Ben Carson. Something happened to Ted Cruz along the way that he needs to figure out but Ben Carson is the real deal. It is great to see him as head of HUD. He knows how to pick yourself up from the bootstraps and become a success. What a wonderful man.

He would have been one of our finest Presidents and he is young enough that perhaps one day he still may—after eight great Trump years.

I am very excited that Donald Trump is serious about helping America and Americans. As a nationalist and populist with a few pounds of conservatism, he does have a lot of Republican values but he does not include in his value list the following:

✓ Greed
✓ Wimpiness

✓ Excessive Happiness to please Hillary Clinton & Democrats
✓ Self-servingness
✓ Self-first
✓ No regard for citizen thought
✓ Excuses for lying about campaign promises
✓ Elitism
✓ Establishmentarianism – being a member of government clubs
✓ Hey there's more

I put this list together in a stream of conscious way. President Trump knows that the Republicans did not give a hoot about him or about the country or they would have been rooting for their own nominee. I am pleased to be the author of the hit Amazon and Kindle book "Kill the Republican Party: Bring on the American Party." Donald Trump has nothing to do with this prior writing effort of mine but he is an American first and a Republican second. Boy, does that sound good!

Donald Trump will not only get us our little a railway stub from Florence to Myrtle Beach, he will connect Scranton and Wilkes-Barre PA and he will connect both of them to NY and Philadelphia and then watch commerce roll literally between all parts of the system.

He will also be building your favorite rail connection so that your city too can be part of the new industrialized America that president Trump has ready for us now that he is our President. The master builder loves to build and he will build an America that nobody in this, our failing period, would ever have imagined. God bless President Donald Trump and keep him safe for America.

Let's take just another break before we get to look at the trains of America so that we can learn how to use Amtrak passenger resources to take us to Myrtle Beach and points south in the USA. And, how about High Speed Rail coast to coast from Washington to San Francisco with two stops in between for pickups and drop-offs.

To gain a perspective at the highest level, let's take a look at the absolute best train system in the world, located in Europe and operating every day for years and years and years.

As part of this section, let's also make note that the up and coming Chinese and Japanese rail systems are some of the fastest in the world. Then, in the bog book when we move to Section II, we will examine the US system and how to use the Amtrak of today to get to Myrtle Beach and points south. We'll also introduce you to the Auto Train, which is a great idea and also very practical. I love the Auto Train. So, does my car. On the auto train, your car gets the night off.

Eurail is phenomenal

The European passenger rail system, which most call Eurail is the finest in the world so let's start there. Just like Amtrak, the American passenger rail system, it does not make a profit. However, its expense is manageable and strategic for the many connected countries. The fact is that anybody who travels the European passenger rail system is treated to innumerable destinations, great rolling stock, and great service. By examining the European passenger rail system, we can know how great the US system can become with the Master Builder in charge.

There is a flip side of the European train story as over time, they have not paid as much attention to cargo as the US profit making train haulers have done. As great as the passenger train system is in Europe, and many, including myself, have fallen in love with it, our cargo haulers carry a substantially higher proportion of freight by train than does Europe. And, the big freight train companies in the US make a lot of money on it, to boot.

One of the reasons why US citizens do not seem to care about having a great train system in America is that most of the country has no passenger service at all. Few people ever miss anything that they have never had. One trip to Europe and a few rides on its trains, and an American will be asking the question of the day: "Why can't we do this in America?"

The answer of course is that we could if we chose to do so. Just as the Europeans must credit a wise and thoughtful set of governments that cooperate to make passenger train travel very comfortable, and a great alternative to air, we can blame our government for the state of affairs in our passenger train industry.

Why travel by train?

Using the European system, which provides excellent passenger services, it is safe to say that rail would be a preferred mode of travel in the US if the system were even half as good as the one in Europe. When the distance is short between stops, the European trains provide fast, reliable and frequent service. When the distance is longer and perhaps traversing multiple countries, the European trains can be preferable even to flying. There are a number of reasons for this.

Airplanes, even big airplanes are cramped and people are loaded in as sardines in a can.

Trains are far more spacious and they are designed with comfortable interiors. Instead of being above the clouds, train travel includes many scenic routes. Moreover, there are not long lines or long waits in the stations as each train car has its own entrance. Trains arrive and "take off," sometimes all within several minutes.

Security is not like that in airports because trains do not get blown up frequently, and they never fall from the sky. The fact that trains run more frequently and in many ways operate for the convenience of the passengers and not the convenience of the airline, makes the overall experience even more appealing and far more pleasant than the entire airport and USA TSA scene.

Figure 1-1 The Plane Sardine Look

Trains take their travelers to railway stations located in or very close to city centers, whereas most airports are from ten to twenty miles or more away from the cities, which they service. Consequently, even before you board the airplane, there is a lot of work just getting to the airport. In Europe, many people may choose the train over the plane for the feeling of romantic travel, which it provides, as well as the personal freedom of being in control of the traveling experience.

Passenger train service in the United States is not as good as in Europe but there is always hope if one day we get the right government in place. US travel is not quite as nice as Europe and the locales serviced are few and far between.

The superiority of foreign train systems over the US is not lost on Presidential Candidate Donald Trump. In what many have labeled a "freewheeling" on a Thursday in March 2016, then

Republican frontrunner Donald Trump found himself talking about how great trains are. Democrats are for trains and Republicans are for big trucks and airplanes. I like Trains myself and it is an embarrassment that we are so far behind.

Trump said "It's sad that the American rail system is so dilapidated while China's is now slicker than ever…They have trains that go 300 miles per hour while we have trains that go chug … chug … chug." Donald Trump sees it and he says it. He is 100% right and you can bet that part of Trump's reindustrialization of America (RRRRRR) will include train manufacturing and lots of high speed rail.

The European rail system consists of 30 different countries with major league rail service. The UK is not part of the Eurail system per se but it does connect. In the UK system alone, there are 21,000 miles of railroad track, which is about the total track used for Amtrak in the US.

The total of the track in the US managed by Amtrak for passenger service as noted is just 21,000 miles. This gives a proper perspective as to how far behind the times we really are in rail, and why European service seems so good in comparison. You cannot run passenger trains without passenger track. As we all know, the UK is much smaller than the US.

When you experience the quality of the European passenger rail system, you know what we in the US are missing. I am surprised that Amtrak actually manages things as well as it does when you consider the overall minimal support it receives from a disinterested government. Even Democrats which talk a big story do not put their money where their mouths are.

Most Americans who have never been to Europe and therefore have never witnessed the efficient and seamless train system connecting almost thirty separate countries, think that excellent regional service and adequate cross country rail service in the

US is impossible to achieve. Our political leaders reinforce this with their negative talk. You'd swear that America can't make anything or operate anything anymore. This is far from the truth. It will take a great man with vision such as Donald J. Trump to get America's passenger rail system back on track.

Our problem in the US is that our government does not have the proper perspective on rail and consequently, no national leaders before Trump have emerged to assure that America does its best in this area. Amtrak as an enterprise is a far better run organization and a smoother running cheetah, when compared with the inefficient US government at large.

The negative insights provided about full-scale rail service in the US are the same kind of rhetoric we have been getting for fifty years or more about energy. In all of our energy emergencies over these years, we have been told that if we began drilling today, it would be at least ten years and maybe fifteen before we had any extra oil / energy. So, when will we begin?

Each year over those fifty years, our country, without real leadership, chose never to start the job. No job can ever be finished before it is begun. And, so we depend on others for energy and we depend on the airlines for interstate distance travel instead of having our own fine-tuned rail / train system. How's the TSA been working out for you lately? Would a nice, comfortable, non-threatening train not serve us all well?

We in the US even depend on others today to build locomotives for our Amtrak system because America seemingly can no longer do even that. For a number of years GE, the major builder of freight locomotives in the USA, would take contracts from Amtrak and Canada to build locomotives to their specifications, but lately Amtrak has been looking overseas for its locomotives.

My hope is that eventually our government in a non-partisan way will see the light and endorse a strategic rail system in the USA. GE and EMD (Electro-Motive Diesel Inc), now a major division of Caterpillar; are two US manufacturers who could do the passenger rail job for sure.

Heck, rather than have the Chinese build our stuff, we could probably get Lockheed Martin, General Dynamics, Northrop Grumman, Raytheon, or maybe even Boeing to build a locomotive plant and make money on it to boot. Politicians think we can't. Remember the old saying that when you think you can't; you're right!

The dollars involved in all facets of rail, both passenger and freight are huge. For the dollars involved, I think I could figure out how to build a plant and put out some pretty spiffy locomotives myself. And, as each one passed the finish line, I would have a party, and yes, there would be beer served, and singing would be permitted. Halleluiah!

They say that haste makes waste. Yet, because the Chinese are in the locomotive and rail business big time, and they gave a super proposal to California, a state that appears to be part of the USA at its convenience, California originally gave them the state's high-speed rail concession. The on-again, off-again project may use China to get the job done.

So, now, a high-speed rail line possibly coming to California by 2029, the Chinese may be major beneficiaries. They have offered to build and run the system. Why California plans to have China build their system some believe is beyond reason. The US can do this and surely if rail is to have a resurgence, US industry must come up to speed, if you will pardon the pun.

With the right funding, I know I can do better if I were in control of the train system in America. We just need to find the right people and motivate them to get the work done, and of course we must do all that is necessary in-between.

Though the California to Nevada line was canceled, a California High-Speed Rail mini-system is supposedly being built. Yes, it is currently under construction in the state of California. The initial implementation phase (Phase 1) will connect the Anaheim Regional Transportation Intermodal Center in Anaheim with the Transbay Transit Center in San Francisco via the Central Valley with speeds up to 220 miles per hour (350 km/h), providing a "one-seat ride" for the trip in 2 hours and 40 minutes. Other than the recent record breaking Japanese trains, 220 mph is as fast as Europe's best high speed systems.

The California system is required by law to operate without a subsidy, and to connect the state's major cities in the Bay Area, Central Valley, and Los Angeles Basin. Phase 2, which has not been designed for implementation yet, would extend the system northerly in the Central Valley to the Sacramento Valley Station in Sacramento, and southerly—through the Inland Empire to the San Diego International Airport in San Diego. The project is managed by CHSRA (the California High-Speed Rail Authority), a state agency run by a board of governors. Who really knows?

Construction on the initial section from Merced to Bakersfield began in 2015 and is expected to end in 2019, after which the Amtrak San Joaquin train is proposed to first use the HSR tracks for faster conventional rail service until HSR trains use the line to its full potential.

Though it is a good idea to use the expertise of the Chinese in building early high speed rail systems, there is no reason why the designers and the implementers and the workers of a functional system cannot eventually all be Americans. We can do it with American labor and ingenuity. Those of us, who know how great train travel can be, know how vital a great train system is to our National interests.

Why settle for adequate, when we are the richest country on earth. Exceptional people can make exceptional products and can provide exceptional operations. Let's start spending our dollars on things that give us a real return. And, yes, while we are building our rail system, let's start building our own passenger locomotives, and all the other wonderful and fashionable train cars that we see in Europe.

Electric locomotives are built outside the US because it appears there are no American companies that produce purely electric locomotives, though some test locomotives have been built. The reason for the high cost of passenger locomotives is because they are produced in limited quantities. Siemens, a well-oiled German corporation has assembly plants in the US to finish off products destined for the US marketplace.

If Siemens would build a lot more of the internal passenger locomotive parts here, I would be happy enough to give Siemens all the business if their technology were the best. Of course, if Caterpillar's EMD Division or GE's train division chose to take on the challenge, if I were the CEO of Amtrak, they would have the upper hand.

America is designed for American's first!

To refresh its aging rolling stock and engines, Amtrak periodically places large orders such as one for big passenger locomotives from Siemens in Europe. One would expect the Europeans to be best in passenger railroad technology but it would be nice if US industry chose to compete, especially when Amtrak, the legal monopoly for rail passenger service in the US is the buyer. The facts indicate that because we do not even know how to buy locomotives in the US, we could have gotten three locomotives for the price of one is we were paying attention. President Trump will not let the US be taken.

Since we are in an introductory chapter (in the big Myrtle Beach book) about the trains of Europe, let's close this part of a whining chapter with c'est la vie. My point in the whining is that America can become productive in heavy manufacturing again if we choose to do so, and we can create a grand passenger railroad system that would help our economy immensely. Think of the engineers across the world, who would like to live in this country. And I am not just talking about those that drive the trains. Casey Jones would be fine but Einstein Jones would be better.

We can bet with President Donald Trump's plans to create more US engineers in our colleges and his serious attitude towards US manufacturing, when elected, President Trump will usher in a new era of rail transportation that we will never forget.

Rail Passes in Europe Are Fantastic

One of the most fascinating aspects of the European Rail System is that all countries cooperate and it appears and behaves externally as one system, not thirty. I would think we should be able to get the lower 48 states to behave in a similar fashion since there is already one federal government that can be used to coordinate efforts.

If you go to Europe and you want to travel by train you can get a pass that permits you to go to any country except Great Britain (UK). The pass is called a Eurail pass. However, if you choose to use the trains in England, Wales, Scotland, and Northern Ireland, with your Eurail pass, you can get as much as a 37% discount on your BritRail pass. Figure 1-1 shows the map of the countries participating in Eurail.

Figure 1-1 Countries Participating in Eurail

For those with bad eyes like me that need to see these countries in a larger type; here goes. These are the Eurail countries and destinations that are part of the Eurail system:

- Austria
- Belgium
- Bulgaria
- Croatia
- Czech Republic
- Denmark
- Finland
- France
- Germany

- Greece
- Hungary
- Ireland (Republic of)
- Italy
- Luxembourg
- Montenegro
- Netherlands
- Norway
- Poland
- Portugal
- Romania
- Serbia
- Slovakia
- Slovenia
- Spain
- Sweden
- Switzerland

If the Europeans can coordinate this between and among countries, it would be a much easier system to operate with the cooperation of the mainland states of our country. We might even build an Alaska line with our partner Canada.

If you are under 26 years of age, as I was on my first trek to Europe, your pass will be lots cheaper than an adult pass. There are lots of other train passes available depending on your needs. The URL below provides a link to a comprehensive chart of all the various passes available. Using these passes, you can book the least expensive and the nicest train journeys possible through Europe.

http://www.eurorailways.com/kb/articles/rail_passes_chart.htm

Every aspect of the European train system is done well. From the first time, you go into a train station, you will be impressed. In fact, even before you go in to your first train, you will be pleased that the European train stations are always conveniently located near the towns they serve.

Additionally, there is a full range of services available at major train stations including lockers, car rentals, souvenir stores, fast foods, wine and beer stores, restaurants. At most locations, there are other reasonable hotels less than a block away. When I was a youngster, I used this fact to book hotels on the day of my arrival in Europe.

Some train stations are even equipped with their own hotel. When you experience this train system, you will conclude that all of this coordination and convenience did not happen overnight and by accident. It was planned well, and implemented well.

There are local trains and regional trains and long distance trains. There are trains that ask you to go over large bodies of water by transferring your person onto a ferry boat, and there are also trains, which are loaded onto huge boats without you having to ever get off the train. Additionally, there are trains that will get you from London to Paris in just a few hours as the train goes under the English Channel. The Eurostar is one such high speed train and it is shown in Figure 1-2 in this insert from a European ticketing web site.

In Figure 1-3, there is a nice picture shown of a huge passenger train going through the beautiful regions of Switzerland. Can you imagine the views from this train?

Figure 1-2 Eurostar from London to Paris

Go from London to Paris:
Fares start at $57

Travel seamlessly from city center to city center within Belgium, France and Britain. Few can match Eurostar's standards for quality of service. Why not ensure the best deal by booking your tickets as soon as possible to get advance purchase discounts?

Book your Eurostar tickets today

Figure 1-3 Switzerland Beauty

Typical train configurations

You can't really tell from the picture above but there are all kinds of train cars in Europe and the United States. There are baggage cars, bar cars, diner cars, sleeper cars, couchette cars, etc. Some European trains still have the old-fashioned couchette configuration, which is very impressive, especially for a first-time traveler. They offer spaciousness and a level of privacy.

As shown above in Figure 1-4, each couchette configured car has a corridor along one side, lined with windows on the outside and doors on the other. In between the doors outside the compartment and the aisle windows, are little round seats attached to the outside of the compartments. These seats spring back to the up position when unoccupied. They come in real handy when a train is overbooked. From my experience, overbooking is more likely to happen in Italy than any other European country.

Figure 1-4 Six seat couchettes together as three beds

Back in my youth (24 yrs. old), when a Eurail train was not highly booked, three travelers could gain a compartment such as the one shown in Figure 1-4, and if no other passenger chose to enter the compartment, it was very easy to claim six seats. Since individually the seats collapsed forward, as you can see in the picture, they became the equivalent of a three-person sleeper car. For young people, this is a great deal, and wherever in the Euro train system it is still offered, this is still a great deal.

Walking down the aisle of a couchette car, you can see ten doors opening into the 10 couchettes. A couchette with the seats folded down is shown in Figure 1-4. Americans would call these compartments. The couchettes would seat six to eight people (or, in first-class compartments, four to six people with slightly cushier chairs.)

The Eurail pass can be purchased to include first class service. Some think it is not worth the added expense even if you have the option. If you hope to get a good night's sleep on a train, I would suggest going for the extra space.

Reservations

When I was twenty-four years old, I did not care as much about comfort as I did convenience and timeliness. With a flexible itinerary, I never knew when I would be leaving a country so reservations were not a good idea to remain flexible. This gave my two friends and I, an immense sense of freedom to hop on many trains on a whim, using our individual rail pass.

Train reservations are now required on many fast, long-distance, international, or overnight European trains, but if there is room, and sometimes, even if there is not, you still may be able to get on and be OK. It may not be comfortable standing but you may still get on. Today, they limit the number of slots for rail pass holders on certain trains, so it is always best to ask the rules at the station in case there are differences between trains or countries.

As you can see when you compare Figure 1-5 with Figure 1-6 on the next page, the modern first class train cars are equipped with bigger and more comfortable seats. This is similar to Amtrak Business Class. Eurail pass travelers over age 26 must buy first class passes while those under26 may also buy second class, which is much cheaper. Senior citizens can opt for the second class less expensive seating also.

Figure 1-5 First Class Rail – Modern Seating.

Three Photos courtesy of www.reidsguides.com

Figure 1-6 Second-Class Seating—not too shabby

As you can see from the difference in seating, second class seats can be very desirable because they often cost one-third less than first class for about ¼ less the space. However, as we get older, first class is worth the price. Riding first class is a lot less crowded; it is much more comfortable. First-class rail passes generally add about 25% to 40% to the price, and so they are a good deal for those seeking comfort.

My favorite train accommodations of all time are the couchettes. Unfortunately, as these wear-out, they are being replaced by more modern straight seating on most train systems. Unfortunately, most short-run trains and even newer high-speed long-haul trains, are being configured with these modern straight-through configurations that run down both sides of an open aisle with no privacy—even in Europe.

For me, they feel more like the regional US trains. It is a lot more like being with those commuting to work than traveling in Europe on a grand vacation. Maybe somebody one day we will all say: "that's enough progress—bring back the couchettes."

Regarding reservations, as noted previously, you also must reserve any sleeping couchette or sleeping room before you board the train. These cost extra. In most cases, you can do this a few hours before your train's departure, but it is always better to play it safe and reserve your spot at least a few days in advance.

One major caution that I would like to add is that even if you think the water is fine on the train, do not drink it. Just as the water may be clean on ships, though it is reconstituted from liquid waste on the ships, nobody suggests you drink it. Don't drink the water on the trains!

Depending on your class of service, you may get water bottles, but as I recall from my travel days there are not too many amenities on the European trains unless you are paying big-time. Don't even brush your teeth or rinse quickly with the water. Then, you will never have to say you are sorry.

High Speed Rail for President Trump's USA

Reach for the moon; do not let go and eat some green cheese for a while. Can you imagine the revenue hit the airlines would take with the overly pleasant TSA in charge, if there were an acceptable train ridership opportunity as an alternative? Why should Americans have to fly to go long distances within the US?

In the Northeast and Southeast, Amtrak is a profitable entity, whereas in the rest of the country, it is mostly a non-entity. What if it were different? President Donald Trump knows how to build big projects and he knows how to run businesses and as a government leader he would know the support that rural American would needs to be able to join the Trump Train!

Transcontinental passenger railway travel in the US would change all that. It does exist really exist without hitting Chicago first. It is not the best and it requires switching trains in Chicago or perhaps New Orleans to go cross-country.

It takes more than 80 train hours from Washington DC to San Francisco on the current Amtrak lines when you switch trains in Chicago. No matter what your choice may be, you have to learn to like train food, or brown bags, and you have to have an awful lot of time.

I would propose building two sets of high speed rail lines directly from Washington to San Francisco (Emeryville, CA. perhaps) with no more than wo stops across the country at about 1/3 distance each. Anticipating future success, I would try to purchase the rights-of-way for a wider bed than just four rail lines. This would be a fully new set of rails, 100% independent of the freight rail lines. It would be designed to have no intersecting tracks for safety reasons other than, of course within the three stations.

At about 2500 miles' distance coast to coast, this would permit Acela type sets of trains / track (used for the US highest speed rail from / to Boston & Washington today) to travel at least 72 MPH. This type of train would arrive in San Francisco in about 35 hours. It should be lots better than that with higher grade tracks and trains. As CEO, I would make it much better. I would build it to accommodate the fast Japanese and Chinese trains.

The tracks across the country can be completed using the full high speed rail quality definition, which would enable trains to travel at least 150 mph. This level of track would support coast to coast travel by train with the right rolling stock in just 16 hours. If the advanced French technology were deployed, the train could go coast to coast at 173 mph and arrive in 14 hours.

Before committing to the specs for the construction of the rail system, I would want to see the future engineering designs of track systems to support high speed rail. If a track system can be built to support even higher speed capabilities of the future that is the goal for which we should shoot.

Considering that the current low tech Amtrak route from Washington to Miami results in a 27-hour ride, 14 or 16 hours to go cross-country is not too shabby! Considering that air travel is about six hours, if you can get a non-stop flight or about 10 hours for a direct one stop flight, 14 or even 16 hours coast to coast train timings would influence a lot of people to choose Amtrak v US Airways to go cross-country. Overall, in fact, more and more people would be traveling. Oh! I forgot to mention that there would be no three-hour TSA wait for security clearance.

Direct High Speed Rail coast to coast from Washington to San Francisco could be a great opportunity for the US. It would only be the start. Soon, the US would be number one in rail. Such a system would have a real big shot at immediate success if managed well, and if all of the political class backed the initiative.   The Master Builder can pull this off.

One last thought. The Shanghai Maglev tops the list of speed trains as the fastest train in the world with its maximum operational speed of 430km/h aka 267 miles per hour.

If we take 2500 miles and divide it by 267, we get 9.3 hours from Washington DC to San Francisco. This speed cannot be maintained 100% for sure. But, as more technology comes in, I can see cross country in eight hours. Can you imagine that. I bet the master builder can do that—President Donald J. Trump. How about Florida in less than three hours?

Chapter 11 The Trump Plan Solves the Student Debt Crisis

Solution for new student debt and the existing $1.3 Trillion debt accumulation

President Donald Trump in simple terms has netted out the student debt crisis from a both a student and parent perspective: "They go, and they work, and they take loans, and they're borrowed up, and they can't breathe, and they get through college and the worst thing is, they go through that whole process and they don't have any job." Trump has it right on and worse than that. They lose hope.

President Trump really cares and he took the time recently to excoriate the Obama Administration and government for making it worse by making money on the student loan program: "You know the one program that the U.S. makes a whole lot of money with is student loans, and that's maybe the one program they shouldn't be making money with... "So, we're going to have to start a program," he said. "We're going to do something very big with loans because you have to get these people going. They really feel down and out."

President Donald J. Trump feels the pain and is going to solve the problem by refinancing, extending, better payment plans, getting universities to take some skin in the matter, and several other clever ways. He will address both the massive $1.3 Trillion student debt already on the books and he will work to assure that students have a chance of success and a chance for a job when they take out a college loan. It's about time. The book titled *The Trump Plan Solves the Student Debt Crisis* tells you how he plans to do it. The book is available on Amazon and Kindle.

Rarely does a book title explain exactly what a book is about. This is the exception. The Trump Plan solves the student debt crisis. Period... It is in fact the solution for new student debt so that new high school aspirants to college do not sign up for debt when they do not need to do so. The plan also addresses how to trim to zero the $1.3 Trillion debt accumulation using some student resources and a few tricks that only a guy like President Donald Trump would know how to do.

Why this book?

Brian W. Kelly wrote this book about Student Loans because he cares about college graduates being able to move on with their lives. Brian has three children with college loans and wishes he could pay them off tomorrow. This book identifies the most notable and most serious flaws in student tuition financing. It then solves them by prescribing a number of Trump-unique solutions to help get the program back on track.

Donald Trump Final Countdown on Student Loans

Donald Trump is a businessman and knows how to solve business problems. He knows that loans cannot be repaid when the borrower (student) cannot find a job. The Trump Plan as we have discussed to solve the student loan debt crisis begins by creating jobs in the private sector. Trump said: "I don't want to raise the minimum wage. I want to create jobs so people can get much more than that, so they can get five times what the minimum wage is," What college graduate wants to work for $15.00 per hour? It is ridiculous.

I have examined a number of Trump notions that would almost immediately solve the student loan debt crisis. None of those solutions suggest that the American taxpayer eat the debt.

Student Loan Forgiveness Programs

Even my children, who are up to their ears in college debt are not looking for forgiveness. They got their degrees. They know they have to pay but with the job market as it is, they would like to be able to pay back their loans on a plan that is affordable. How about the usury interest charges payable to Obama over the last years that are lots more than the 1% that their parents earn on their income? Trump likes that plan. He thinks Obama and company should not have made a dime off the student's backs.

By improving the job market as the Trump plan ensures, borrowers, such as my children would be able to afford their payments rather than using their deferment and forbearance options until they expire. Perhaps President Trump will elect to use the profits of the Obama Student Loan takeover to initiate some loan forgiveness programs as well as offering relief to student borrowers who need immediate relief.

Few Americans, especially other students who paid off their debt with no help, think student loan borrowers should have their debt 100% forgiven. But for God sakes, how about a plan that lets them pay as much as they can and lets them get credit against the principal so that their largest bequethment, when these, who are so indebted finally die, is not their debt.

Trump's Position on Student Loans

Yes, Donald Trump has a position on student loans. While some say that Trump has been extremely vague about his plans for student loans if elected, here's what we do know so far:

Trump has stated that he does not want the federal government profiting from student loans any longer (and blames government for driving up tuition costs)

He thinks the Department of Education could "largely be eliminated," but did not elaborate on how the $28 billion spent on Pell Grants for students would be affected. He will make sure students and millennial graduates are OK!

He wants to restructure student loans but says government "can't forgive these loans" outright...

He wants to return student lending to private banks and away from the federal government (in order to improve salary data and allow students to make more informed decisions about whether the tuition costs are worth it)

He proposed tying new student loan decisions to the borrower's future job prospects, an assessment likely based on the student's major.

He wants to punish colleges and universities who have not delivered to students financially when their students fail to repay their loans, adding that he wants colleges themselves to have "skin in the game" and would be on the hook if too many of their former students defaulted on their loans...and had no jobs. If Colleges cannot assess a student's prospects for success, perhaps they should not be permitted to grant loans at all.

President Trump wants colleges to set more stringent standards for who is admitted, denying access to those it deems unlikely to succeed. Everybody should have the right to pay up front with no loan and not be a financial burden on the rest of us.

Most of the issues covered in this book for hook or for crook are the way Donald Trump would solve them. If you do not believe so, let us know the issue and we will ask Mr. Trump to comment!

Trump knows for sure!

President Donald Trump can recognize a rigged game better than any man in America. He can sniff them out and call them out and /or play against them and still win. He thinks the student loan game is rigged against students and it favors the universities and the loan sharks. He is 100% correct!

Trump does not like that it is rigged and he promises to fix it.

President Trump was the only presidential candidate who had the US student loan debt crisis solved on both fronts. His plan addressed both new student loans and the $1.3 trillion in accumulated student debt. He is serious about it and like all Trump solutions, there will be no pandering to special constituencies. Universities must have some skin in the game for long term solutions to be built properly.

Many people are affected by the crisis and so it is a topic at the dinner table in many homes—especially in those homes in which the student loan invoices are beginning to arrive for junior's or missy's four or five-year sojourn into academia.

When people in the US discuss the student debt crisis, most focus on how it affects them personally. If they are not directly affected, they discuss the rapid growth in outstanding debt and its impact on the economy and the country.

They may also discuss some of the recent milestones, which are not very positive. For example, student loan debt exceeded credit card debt in 2010 and it exceeded auto loan debt in 2011. It is rapidly rising and it passed the $1 trillion mark in 2012. It is currently at about $1.3 Trillion and growing. It is a big problem.

With about 27% of students defaulting on their loan paybacks mostly because the payments are too large, it is a problem for all America. It is a big disgrace for a country that does not want to be labeled as "Third World." We can do better with our students, for sure.

These milestone financial numbers do not tell us much about the impact of all that debt on the students themselves. They were originally made to believe by their friendly Financial Aid Officer that everybody borrows and it is a privilege to be able to attend this college with the help of the university's loan package.

Nobody looked at their SATs and their HS transcript and gave them a probability of success in college and a probability of success in the outside world. This must be done before any loan is signed.

Sometimes as learned from students in loan default interviews, there was no up-front discussion of the loan impact. Thus, 53% of the students when graduating, did not even know there was a payback. And we all know what payback is!

70% of all college students have borrowed or still must borrow to pay for their college education. It is a national travesty. America had been told by Team Obama when he ran things that we are not exceptional. The way his government treated the best and the brightest Americans, who simply were not well enough fortified to pay the huge tuition bills of today, is proof that this president and his administration were not kidding, nor did they care.

Meanwhile Obama picked up $billions in profits from scobbing students with high government interest rates. No matter how immune you get to hearing about government $billions here and there, remember that a $billion is an extremely large amount of money.

Even a $million is quite large. A million is so big it gives more meaning to the word billion. It is 1000 million. Would you not like to have a $million right now?

Obama's government made the problem worse for student loan debtors by taking more money for loans than the government needed. Uncle Sam is on track to make $66 billion in profits after Uncle Obama took over the student loan program six years ago. That's why Donald Trump wants to turn the program back over to private enterprise at competitive rates. Why should Obama have permitted hurting students to be further hurt by excessive government interest.

Average student loan debt at graduation is still getting larger and larger over the last two decades. In 1993-94, the average debt was just $10,000. Now, about 70% of college graduates are saddled with huge debt. Their average debt at the time they get their sheepskins is now about $35,000. It has tripled in two decades.

Graduate school debt is even worse at well over $100,000 per student. If most students were getting high paying jobs as in the past, the problem would not be as severe as students would be able to pay back the loans. Bartenders have a tough time handling Obama approved government repayment rates.

Why is student debt increasing? Government under Democrat control with grants and support for postsecondary education have simply chosen not keep pace with increases in college costs. Democrats have sold out American-born College students to gain the favor of the universities.

Government money has been diverted to welfare programs and other schemes that give Democrats advantages when they appear at fringe group events as Santa Claus. Democrats have forgotten completely about white America and the students from white America who are now saddled with huge debt repayment plans.

This is not a racist thing. It is a fact. It simply is a bunch of overzealous white Democratic Congressmen thinking they can get the black vote by stiffing their white constituency. I am color neutral but I notice things.

Colleges are oblivious as nothing has been able to hurt them. They are making money every year on the taxpayer's back. They make another ton of money each year while students and graduates scrounge for alms. This is the college and university renaissance period. They get to build new theatres, art museums, student centers, gymnasiums, and all kinds of amenities to attract students and making their campuses more beautiful to the eye.

They need money to build, and to heat these fine edifices to their success. So, the burden of tuition financing has shifted much of the burden of paying for college from the federal and state governments to families. Meanwhile the drive to become the college with the finest amenities has pushed tuition charges through the roof.

Since grants and gifts and scholarships simply are not there anymore thanks to the Democrats in Congress, various types of loans in the "package" have become the primary vehicle today for high school students to make the jump to college. What does a high-school kid know about the financing necessary for college? Nothing!

The government no longer carries its fair share of college costs, even though it gets a big increase in income tax revenue from college graduates who are fortunate enough to get jobs.

Ironically when the first loan bill comes to the home address after a college graduation or dropout; first the parents, then the students are shocked that they owe so much money. Worse than that, they become convinced at the wording of the invoice that they must pay it back. Somehow, until the risk of the student withdrawing from the institution is long past, nobody from the university finds it necessary to talk about the real cost of those loans.

In the Obama economy and even for several years before, while the President had a majority Democratic Congress, family income has been flat and for many it has gone down. There is not a lot of money to pay for frills such as education.

Therefore, students have been forced to either borrow more to pay for college or enroll in lower-cost colleges, or forego completely entering an opportunity for a dream life. Without Santa Claus, work is a necessary ingredient in everything.

That shift in enrollment, from private colleges to public colleges and from four-year colleges to two-year ones, has also been responsible for a decline in bachelor's degree attainment among low and moderate-income students.

Why have Democrats in Congress who love all people not solved this? Can it be that they feel they would be helping the white privileged and they might risk reelection from their diverse constituencies? You tell me!

If numbers could speak, what would they be saying?

In a recent policy paper that I read, student loan debt was defined as affordable if [Big IF] half of the after-tax increase in income that a student gains from obtaining a college degree is sufficient to repay that student's loans in 10 years or less. Nice try.

What if the student cannot get a job that uses his or her degree no matter what the student does, and they wind up being the local bartender for 20 hours per week? Before we fall off the face of the earth on that notion, let's look at what the numbers might say.

Suppose the average starting salary for a bachelor's degree recipient in the humanities discipline is about $45,000 as noted by the National Association of Colleges and Employers. That figure compares with about $30,000 in average income for high-school graduates—or a $15,000 difference.

After considering taxes, the net increase for attending college and taking all the risks is about $9,000. Half of that ($4,500) is about 10% of gross income and would be enough to repay roughly $35,000 in student loans over a 10-year repayment term. This works if the policy paper thesis is operative. It is consistent with the rule of thumb that says total student loan debt at graduation should be less than the borrower's annual starting salary.

If we accept this as a definition of affordable debt, we can analyze the data from the Baccalaureate & Beyond Longitudinal Study and we would find that the percentage of bachelor's degree recipients graduating with excessive debt grew from 9.8% in 1993-94 to 14.4% in 2007-08. Let's say the percentage has continued to grow at the same rate to today. This would suggest that 16.7% of college graduates are now graduating with excessive debt. But, it sure seems like the real percentage is a lot higher—at least per the default rate.

Why? Part of the reason is that even this percentage underestimates the bigger problem. It includes all students who graduate with a bachelor's degree—even those without any debt at all. Suppose we were to look only at students who borrowed to attend college. It appears that more than a quarter (27.2%) of them would be and in fact are graduating with excessive debt. Some statistics show the number at closer to 30%

Can indebted students ever get back their lives?

If President Obama had spent less time on the ill effects of white privilege and the positive purposes of black lives matter, perhaps, just perhaps, he might have had time in eight years to have analyzed and fixed the student debt problem. Maybe he thinks it is a white-only problem and white people will solve it without his help. I do not know as Obama is an enigma. What do I know?

The fact is Team Obama has had no ammunition at their disposal to solve any problem that presents itself with facts and/or numbers. Now the problem I left to President Trump. I for one think that is good. He has big shoulders.

Even in his trusted Cabinet and his trusty Czars, which the media is no longer permitted to acknowledge, but who still exist, there were no business majors. There were no MBA's. There was nobody who knew anything about capitalism and how it really works. No wonder Obama failed to solve the problem.

These pompous partial humans look down on capitalism and those trying to eke out a living in business. They innately know that they have all the knowledge as great elites always have. Why would they need to bring in an expert to solve any problem that their limited skills should dictate?

I diverted to this several paragraph diatribe because former President Barack Obama and Trump's opponent Hillary Clinton are one and the same in terms of understanding business and how to make things run. If Obama and Hillary could have solved it before today, unless they hate America, they would have solved it, right?

I know Donald Trump can and will solve it Looking at the report introduced in the beginning of this chapter. You would soon find that students who graduate with excessive debt are about 10% more likely to say that it caused delays in their major life events, such a buying a home, getting married, or having children. T

hey are also about 20% more likely to say that their debt influenced their employment plans, causing them to take a job outside their field, to work more than they desired, or to work more than one job.

Perhaps not surprisingly, they are also more likely to say that their undergraduate education was not worth the financial cost. Get out of town! What do universities say about that? Nobody in the corrupt press is interviewing university presidents on that subject. Why? Because the press is corrupt. But, you already knew that.

Unfortunately, there are no similar studies that can be used to analyze excessive debt for other college degrees, such as associate degrees, certificates, and graduate or professional-school degrees. It is also not possible to evaluate the financial impact of student loan debt on students who drop out of college, even though they are four times more likely to default on their loans.

There is little financial redemption for a college dropout. Maybe that is why we find them as continual lottery players or among those restricted from casinos. Looking for their big break without having a job is a losing proposition.

What Can Be Done?

Increasing national awareness of college spending is the first step in exercising restraint. Congress of course must listen to its constituents. It is therefore imperative that the federal government and the colleges and universities begin tracking the percentage of their students who are graduating with excessive debt each year.

This information can then be used to improve student loan counseling if there actually is such a thing today in universities that want to be the most successful.

Colleges must also be given better tools to limit student borrowing. This is surely true. But, reality says that without federal or state insistence, would these revered institutions of higher learning even use the tools designed to help students if in so doing, they decreased their own financial opportunities to exploit student borrowers into signing up for their huge tuition packages?

Most colleges and universities are aware of the problem and until now, they have checked all their altruistic feelings at the door. One would conclude that if the college could collect one more enrollment, a little truth bending would not be excessive force.

If life were fair for example, college financial aid administrators would be permitted and in fact incented to reduce federal loan limits based on the student's enrollment status and academic major. They choose not to look at the students' prospects for success because they may not get the acceptance rate they desire.

Yes, doing things against the grain would be a lot of work and it might result in less revenue for the institution. Who would suffer? Students who are enrolled half-time simply should not be able to borrow the same amount as students who are enrolled full-time.

But, perhaps college officials get a little back when they sell a lucrative loan package from a private lender to a student who never even should have been admitted. Who really knows?

If colleges and universities had a student-first attitude, they would also help students better understand the debt they are taking on, by making the distinction between loans and grants clearer in their financial aid award letters.

Surprise, 53% of students who get their first loan invoice did not know they owed anything? What does that's say about truth in lending? Where is the Congress? President Donald Trump will solve this problem because he knows how and he loves America more than its prestigious universities.

A gentleman named Mark Kantrowitz is one of the nation's leading student financial aid experts. He is the author of a number of books written for students about paying for college. His works talk about things like Filing the FAFSA, Wisdoms about Paying for College, and Secrets to Winning a Scholarship.

Mark is publisher of Cappex.com, a website that helps students achieve their college dreams, and he previously served as publisher of the FinAid, Fastweb, and Edvisors websites. So what? Well, he just gave us most of the facts in this chapter. Thank you Mark!

One solution: How about a Progressive Loan Payback Schedule

Without getting very complicated, I would recommend putting together a progressive payback schedule (like the progressive income tax) based on adjusted gross income. Every borrower with income or receiving government payments should have to pay something. Nobody should pay less than 1% of their income. But paying 90% of income towards loan debt makes graduates soon decide to default.

I would start the maximum rate of payment at 5% for the lowest income borrowers and then take it up to 15% for those in default who are doing very well. Of course, in no instance would anybody have to pay more than the minimum monthly payment for the loan even if they could afford it.

To help pay for the program, I would also set up a fund for any taxpayer to check off from $1.00 up to any amount on their tax forms to have part of their refund directed towards the paying down of all student loans. We do this for campaign donations so why not for student loans. I have other recommendations and the big book with the same name as the chapter name has the rest of the skinny.

Chapter 12 Seniors, Social Security, & the Minimum Wage, a Trump Perspective

Why do seniors always come in last?

When I first checked out the $15.00 minimum wage proposal for fast food workers, I kept thinking that it would be hard for seniors to "enjoy" fast food ever again. With the pig slop in fast foods, the bright side was that maybe it would help seniors live longer. But, I am quite sure that living longer is not a goal that government has for seniors. Ask our friend Ezekiel Emanuel, one time Obama ethics doctor who made most of the health regulations to help seniors die early.

He is the guy who claims he is seeking to become 75 years old so he can finally die. He also suggests that seniors no longer burden the healthcare system with their needs. Why bother getting physicals every year at such an enormous cost to the government?

One thing I know and you know. When seniors die, after that one measly SS death payment, we are a statistic, not a health burden for guys like Ezekiel Emanuel, an Obama guy. Thank God Trump is healthy at 71. Emanuel would have had him excluded for a second term. Emanuel probably has President Donald J Trump's affordable casket (if needed) already picked out for him.

I do wish the fast food industry was the only victim for the $15.00 per hour national wage. We all want everybody to do as well as they can. So, nobody begrudges the fast food workers who will get $15.00 per hour even though right now the US minimum wage is now $7.25. Even the optimists know that when fast food workers begin making $30,000 per year, at $15.00 per hour, other industry workers will be looking for more in their paychecks.

We all know that if $30,000 ever became the prevailing national yearly wage, what that would do to seniors on a fixed income. Those care providers who make about $20,000 per year do not compete for the fast food jobs today but if it represents a $10,000 pay differential, we may even see college graduate social workers who now take care of many seniors, going for the $15.00 fast food jobs. Flipping burgers may be a far easier job than flipping patients for the inevitable unpleasant cleanup.

As an aside, thank you to those folks who help the elderly and I hope you are paid well.

Then will the fast food workers who may not measure up v the college graduates vying for their jobs try to get the $20,000 social worker jobs? Or should everybody be given the new $30,000 wage? Who knows when government takes over the wage scale.?

If everybody gets the new $30,000 wage, how is it a wage increase because it will merely add to inflation?

I have the answer since Obama has raised the social security wage almost never in his eight years and he plans no increase in 2016, and nobody I know has gotten anything in 2017. It will be seniors who pay for everybody's huge wage increases.

Is that really what Hillary, a huge proponent of a $15.00 min wage increase really wanted? How long can seniors last when everything costs more than double? Surely those paying the

$30,000 per year will be raising prices and seniors will be the only ones not getting raises. Thank you, cheapskate Obama. Thank you, Hillary,? Seniors: don't blame Trump for this one folsk!

The CPI is a big ripoff for seniors

I just took a run out to shadowstats.com, a site run by Walter "John Williams" for years. Williams has figured out something that the government does not want you to know. The Consumer Price Index as calculated by the US Bureau of Labor Statistics is calculated intentionally to produce a lower number than actual. Government lies and it helps them cheat you and I and all seniors out of appropriate cost of living increases.

Please look at the chart below. Look at the line where it says shadow stats.

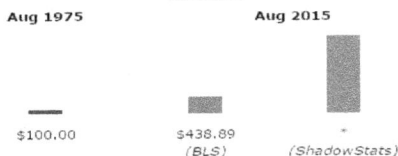

www.shadowstats.com/inflation_calculator/amount1=100&y1=1975&m1=8&y2=2015&m2=8&calc=Find+Out

John Williams' **Shadow Government Statistics**
Analysis Behind and Beyond Government Economic Reporting

| Home | Content Index | Alternate Data | Chart Library | Contact Us | Subscribe |

Inflation Calculator

Enter a dollar amount and two dates.
The second date can be later or earlier than the first.
$100 in 1975 ▼ Aug ▼
was worth how much in 2015 ▼ Aug ▼ ?
Find Out

This Historical Inflation Calculator will calculate the amount of CPI price inflation between any two dates from 1913 up to the latest month reported by the U.S. Bureau of Labor Statistics (BLS).

Aug 1975   **Aug 2015**

$100.00 $438.89   *
                 (BLS)   (ShadowStats)

BLS: Bureau of Labor Statistics, CPI-U (Urban Workers, All Items).
ShadowStats: Shadow Government Statistics Alternate CPI.

* ShadowStats subscribers, please login to view the actual figure

The CPI data is sourced from the BLS. However, we also present our own "Alternate ShadowStats" CPI estimates for comparison purposes.

Further background on the SGS-Alternate CPI series is available in our Public Comment on Inflation Measurement.

Note that we show the Alternate SGS estimates graphically for non-subscribers, and with numerical precision for subscribers.

Also on that same "line," you can see with good eyesight that I typed in $100.00 for the value of the money in 1975. The CPI total of $438.89 is the amount that $100 was worth in August, 2015 after forty years later.

Notice the small bar graph showing this dollar value in graph form on top of the two numbers and on top of the word term ShadowStats. When you look to this right-most bar graph, you would normally see the shadow stats numeric value.

This is John Williams' calculator based on real inflation numbers. I used this fee subscription site for my purposes in this book. I am running low on funds so I did not pay to see the actual number the program produced.

However, the bar graph is proportional. Judging from the size of the graphs, I would estimate the shadow stats CPI (a true CPI without government input) to be about 5X the dollar amount. Let's say the value is $2000.00.

What that means for a senior who began collecting $100.00 per month in 1975, whether in SS cash benefits form or SSI cash benefits form, if there was some honesty in the government, their 2015 number instead of $438.89 would be $2,000. That is a lot of difference in lifestyle. Don't you think?

Some would say that the explanation is quite simple. Our government lies habitually in an institutionalized fashion. It is part of everyday government life. I do not trust the government. Do you?

I wrote John Williams for the actual number for the shadow stats. It would be interesting to have his shadow stats calculator to see the real numbers for the Barack H. Obama years from 2005 to 2016. If you become a member of his site, you can calculate the Obama years impact on your social security yearly benefit. In case you forgot, here are the Obama numbers. I have heard the 2016 numbers would be zero also.

You can tell I have little regard for Obama policies. But, I admit that I liked it when he squared off against Hillary Clinton when he was Senator Barack Obama. Perhaps you remember these fighting words: Sen. Obama pretty much called Clinton a political opportunist, who "would say anything to get elected" and "change nothing." I am not interested in more Obama for sure, and the fact that Hillary promises four more years of Obama policies is enough to drive me to Trump. How about you? For me, I already like Trump because he is the real deal!

Mrs. Clinton was 100% for the $15.00 minimum wage and for children. We are all for children so that gave her nothing. But, she never paused and said, "as well as the elderly." I saw a return of Obama's Chained CPI in the future.

What do you think? Would you trust Obama's hand-picked successor with your presidency? Not me! I thank God that our God cares enough about America that he gave us President Donald J. Trump. Who could ask for anything more.

Who really does take care of Senior Citizens?

This question reminds me of a great "Chicago" song that begins with the words: "Does anybody really know what time it is. Does anybody really care? Does anybody really know what time it is?

If you are really wondering about the heading question for this section, please know that seniors take care of seniors for the most part with a lot of help from juniors who care. When seniors get sick, sometimes the end is near but often it is just a temporary setback.

In both cases, seniors need themselves, their spouses and their families and a lot of other juniors to help out. Most seniors spend an awful lot of time helping seniors when they were juniors. Nothing is expected but that's just the way it is. It's nice to be nice!

That's who takes care of seniors. As a senior, I take care of myself as does my wife but we also take care of each other. It just gets harder every day; especially with a government that chooses not to keep the dollar inflation-proof for seniors.

That's what we want. We want inflation-proof dollars and we do not want to be stiffed by the government. Obama seems to have enjoyed stiffing seniors for most of his years in office. I can't remember him ever saying he was sorry.

Now instead of what is fair for seniors, before President Trump, we had a government that wanted to lie and pretend there was no inflation. This government too often insinuated that seniors were fat cats needing nothing.

Meanwhile, the same government was hoping to legislate the raising of the wages of people who, if you'll pardon me, hold the jobs that have always been intended to be at the lowest wage scale. Why the attention to them, and why not to seniors?

A lot of people would have to give a lot back if retroactively to 1930, the 2016 or 2017 government of the US set a maximum wage that could not be exceeded, and a minimum wage that would hold the line on wages. If there is a minimum, perhaps it is fair that there is a maximum… don't you think?

How is it that all the people outside of we, who are supposed to be protected by senior status are getting major increases in their monthly checks? We seniors ask our kids and our grandkids, why can the government decide that everybody else can make a living wage but those of us who contributed to our own living wage are held captive of a CPI that was invented so that the government would not have to help us be to able to afford next year's expenses.

If the people have given government such power to determine the mins and maxes in their life, then the people cannot blame the founders because the founders' only wish was for freedom. Freedom means no mins and no maxes.

Who should it be to regulate both max and min. It's nobody, that's who! The founders nor the people have ever granted government such powers. The reality is government should not even be a player in our lives as it is a non-contributor to the productivity of society. Government is a detractor.

The fact is that there should neither be a minimum nor a maximum wage dictated by any government, especially the US Republic. If there is a minimum and all the elites in the establishment in Congress want to bring it in as the law of the land, then for fairness, there should also be a maximum. With a maximum, all the members of Congress should be prepared to deposit a lot of their spare cash into the US Treasury or permit themselves to be arrested as we commoners would be. What is fair is fair!

Now, if we were to continue with Chicago's Lyrics to catch the spirit of our times: "If so I can't imagine why, about time--We've all got time enough to cry.

For the last twenty or thirty years post-Reagan, we have all had a lot of time to cry. Both Chicago the City and Chicago the fabulous musical group shown above know that for sure. You can see it in the group's songs.

"And I was walking down the street one day. A pretty lady looked at me and said her diamond watch had stopped cold dead...And I said..."Does anybody really know what time it is...I don't...Does anybody really care...If so I can't imagine why, about time...We've all got time enough to cry."

There we are again talking about crying. Well, I am a senior and I am really tickled about being alive; but I am also ticked about government. I am running out of money for sure as most of us are, whose industry pensions are frozen and whose Social Security, thanks to Barack the Miser Obama did not kept up with the real cost of living. This of course renders the dollars of us seniors to be of much less worth than we would have ever expected.

Of course, all seniors are running out of time and it is much more quickly than juniors, young-ins, infants, and others. We will live however, until we die, and we do not need politicians such as Hillary Clinton, who wanted to make everything more expensive for us by giving the rest of the country minimum wage raises while our lot remains the same. One might think she desired to make our day of doom come sooner. You'll have to ask her if Lester Holt permits you to interrupt her

Senior social security dollars seem to never increase when the Miser in chief, Barack Obama was at the helm. Even if there were ever a token raise, the real cost of living increase we experience as shown in ShadowStats grabs most of it and more; and so it is non-spendable. The real rate of inflation is a never divulged by the government as they are very comfortable lying to the people.

If gas prices go up, they take gas out of the calculation and if gas prices go down, they put gas back in to lower the COLA. The market basket once had steak and when the price got high, they put hamburger in; then tuna, and now cat food that taste like Tuna. How's it feel kitty? I know I don't like it.

We do have enough time to cry but we won't anyway because we grew up differently. I am not crying and I am not complaining. I admit, however, that I did expect that government would be fair—at least when I was younger.

Instead of keeping seniors in our place by using our already invested dollars to help those who are not helpless, it would be nice if government were truthful and properly divulged the inflation rate, rather than substituting the price of 80% hamburger and dog and cat food for the price of a cheap steak in their CPI numbers.

Most seniors would rather the government put the dimes and pennies we place into Social Security into secure coffers intended to help seniors through our later years. Nobody was happy with Obama and company using our Medicare dollars as an example to fund Obamacare. There ought to be a law! Yet, I fear most seniors, especially Democrats find no fault with Obama, the big perpetrator. Instead, the fault the "government."

When you stop trusting government, you might even believe that such minions would give your hard-earned contributions to SS to foreign interlopers simply because they could use a lift. The same minions of course, keep their own wallets out of the divvy picture.

Let's say a dollar has a purchasing power of 30 X's when we put it into the SS system. Now, the value of the same dollar is 15 or less—substantially less. Inflation is the most unfair and unkind tax that government puts on its people, and seniors pay the most in inflation tax.

So, as the musical group Chicago continues: "I was walking down the street one day, being pushed and shoved by people trying to beat the clock, oh, so I just don't know, I just don't know. And I said, yes I said-- People runnin' everywhere; Don't know the way to go; Don't know where I am; Can't see past the next step; Don't have to think past the last mile; Have no time to look around; Just run around, run around and think why does anybody really know what time it is. I don't. Does anybody really care…care…If so I can't imagine why…About time, we've all got time enough to die…Oh no, no."

Especially seniors have time enough to die as death is more frequently on our minds than when we were kids. We've all got time enough to die, don't we? Raising the minimum wage while not compensating seniors via Social Security for the lost purchasing power, won't affect our having time enough to die. We'll still have the time but the time won't be as pleasant. Everybody does have time enough to die or they would all still be living!

Folks, oh, yes, yes, yes, yes! No senior wants to be beholden to government for anything. All seniors know is that the SS deal that those in our family history signed up for in the 1930's was made with an honest government. When SS passed, it was a good deal then but the deal has been broken many times since and we always have to go back to the original intentions.

Our current crooked politicians have soured Social Security as well as Medicare. Democrats use the press to blame Republicans even today for the past eight years of minimal or no raises from Obama himself. Gullible seniors lapped up the news and choose not to blame the former president. It could not have been BHO who stiffed seniors on the COLA…but it was! Hillary was ready to do the same.

IMHO, seniors were misinformed or chose to be low information voters or they loved the Democrat Parts too much to pin failure on them. Trump won seniors clearly but what about the 40% of seniors who voted to give themselves a benefit cut by voting for Hillary?

Establishment Democrats and Republicans in Congress were not ready to commit to seniors. Donald Trump was different. He was clear in his support for seniors' issues like being starved to death by the government.

Candidate Trump appealed directly to the overwhelming senior desire to protect their government benefits. Too bad a lot of seniors ignored his pro-senior message. The need for entitlement reform may be a gospel of today's Republican Party and a hallmark of the budget plans proposed by House Speaker Paul

Ryan. Donald Trump feels differently. But while virtually the entire rest of the Republican field was promising to restore fiscal discipline by reforming Social Security and Medicare, Trump insisted the programs didn't need to be touched.

Now, we call on President Trump to put something back into the pockets of seniors. I feel it is not out of line to suggest t make up for the years of zero raises by Obama that President Trump for the next four years provide a 10% per year COLA, with an emergency outlay beginning this year. After all, nearly half of the seniors out there are somebody's mother!

The corrupt press knows that the actions of the former Democratic President, Barack Hussein Obama, who did not care too much about the elderly has had a harmful effect on all seniors. Yet, their allegiance to Party is still greater than their allegiance to America. If Democrats such as Hillary and Obama wanted t take care of Seniors, we would have heard about it during the 2016 election cycle. So, I send a message to those seniors who supported Hillary. She did not have your back on seniors' issues.

G. Gordon Liddy dollars reflect the proper value

Meanwhile the whole government pretends there is no inflation though the cost of what seniors must purchase to live keeps increasing. Why is it that today it seems that the only people living in America who are not to be compensated for the increases in their cost to live—huge costs that make each dollar smaller, are the most-needy of seniors. Isn't the dollar held by G. Gordon Liddy above the tell-all on inflation?

I am now a sixty-nine-year-old senior with lots of seniors as friends. Who knows how old I will feel tomorrow. Today I feel less than 50. I do however, have that sense of hopelessness some seniors get when sometimes things go bad. But, mostly and I might even say very mostly, I am OK! I thank God, not the government, for that.

Thankfully, I still have a few years left from my industry pension. I have lots of juniors as friends because God still permits me to walk briskly and he still keeps my brain sharp so I can outfox those who want to take from seniors and redistribute to those who should be working in America. That is why I am writing this book—for all seniors. During the election season, I urged all seniors to not vote for anybody who would make it worse for us. In other words, I suggested a vote against Hillary Clinton, whose minimum wage proposal would have hurt all seniors.

I don't think what is happening is fair. Few do; but it is seniors who feel the pain of increasing costs the most. I do not think that when Franklin Roosevelt made the deal with the people, any of the citizens back then, like the seniors of today, who ultimately grew into their retirement years, felt that Roosevelt would cheat them out of their SS payment.

Did Roosevelt plan for government to be saying that a dollar is a dollar even if it is worth less than half of what it was worth in 1930? We know he did not? Why should seniors be paid in Liddy dollars or Roosevelt dollars? Pay us in real dollars.

Every year more and more seniors drop below the poverty level. For example, in 2015, the supplemental poverty report from Census Bureau showed that over 2.3 million more seniors dropped below poverty level. The supplemental poverty rate for example, is 14.6% while the "official Poverty Measure is 9.5 %. If seniors were compensated fairly by Social Security for lost purchasing power from inflation, they would not be dropping into poverty levels so rapidly.

FYI, the official poverty rate is based on pretax money income. The supplemental poverty measure also factors in costs for critical goods and services and government benefits to determine the number of people living in poverty.

The Census Bureau came up with this measurement because the official rate was not properly reflecting the pain out there. Using their new "supplemental poverty rate," the situation is clearly direr. What makes it even worse is that if there were no Social Security, the majority of the total senior population (52.6 percent or 23.4 million) would be among the poverty class. Quite frankly, that is why seniors get so upset when the pure politicians mess with Social Security at any level.

Seniors also suffer from an excessive medical out-of-pocket expense. If the numbers did not account for medical out-of-pocket expenses, instead of the actual 48.7 million in poverty, the number of people below the poverty line would have been 37.5 million.

Being a senior is not an easy thing to do with few sources of income. But, I might also add that being a senior is never having to say you're sorry. Yet, without a proper level of income, no senior can survive. Having all prices rise by providing a $15.00 minimum wage, as proposed by Hillary Clinton, to unskilled workers, with no corresponding increase in take home income for seniors is a recipe for a disaster in the United States that seniors believe is unnecessary. Politicians must make sure that seniors are made whole!

Obama's Sneak Attack on Senior Citizens

I am closing this chapter and this book shortly. To help seniors who love Obama and Hillary understand that the feeling is not mutual, I include a few pages describing a 2012 Forbes article about President Obama's disdain for seniors. We saw it in his unwillingness to give us a raise. This article shows he had planned to make it worse.

The article about President Obama and seniors was titled, Obama's "Sneak Attack" on Senior Citizens. John Marioti was the Forbes Contributor who put the article together.

Figure 3-1. Sneak Attack by a Sneaky Pete

Sections of Mr. Marioti's excellent piece are included below. It is well-written and very telling. The first two paragraphs are shown on the next page. The worst news of all is that things have only gotten worse for seniors since 2012, and with Hillary Clinton's wishing and hoping to continue and step up Obama's lawless dictatorship if she were elected, things would only have gotten worse.

There are a lot of senior citizens in the US now. The number is increasing by 10,000 every day as Baby Boomers turn 65—and start applying for Medicare and then shortly after that, for Social Security [SS]. Some almost oldsters needing cash do the reverse and take their SS early at 62, and Medicare at 65.

These are the folks who once thought this would be their "Golden Years" when years of hard work and savings and pension plans would let them live the good life, in places that are sunny and warm. Not in an Obama or Hillary world for sure. Seniors are now counting on President Trump for major relief.

Then came the financial crisis and the stock market crash, the recession, and the lied about "non-recovery." Whatever "nest egg" they thought they had suddenly was mostly gone. Panicked, they sold their portfolio of securities on the way down, and then fearful of what came next, they didn't buy back in on the way up. Thus, they missed out on the stock market growth over the past 18-24 months. They are left with a much smaller "nest egg," or none at all, and their pensions are either broke or being discontinued too.

I admit that some seniors are not so well off as to have any type of cushion, even a somewhat depleted one. Though many seniors love Obama even as they are eking by after the devastating Obama years, very few hold him as president accountable—even though he caused most of the misery in their personal misery index.

FYI The formal **misery index** is an economic indicator, created by economist Arthur Okun, the **misery index** helps determine how the average citizen is doing economically and it is calculated by adding the seasonally adjusted unemployment rate to the annual inflation rate. Obama is not the only one who can add to the misery index. See picture Figure 3-2. The lady on the right below would have done her own addition to the index if given the opportunity

As bad as that sounds, it's not the "worst news." The "worst news" is that President Barack Obama plans and policies constitute a multi-faceted "sneak attack on seniors." Obama cleverly conceals this "sneak attack" while he assures seniors citizens he's going to take care of them—and "nothing will change" for them. Nonsense!

Figure 3-2 Two Other "Presidents"

It helps to remember presidential aspirant Mrs. Hillary Clinton put the US citizenry on notice that she admired Obama's polices and was ready to continue them. But, her plan was foiled by President Trump.

The Chained CPI was just a nasty Obama trick

Besides the continual understatement of the cost of living leading to no COLA for seniors on Social Security for four out of Obama's eight years, this past President was not content to simply take money directly from the pockets of existing SS recipients. The fully engaged Team Obama were prepared to stiff even new guys who had yet to collect one dime.

For all eight years, Obama, along with special Congressional budget negotiators were looking at proposals to marginalize Social Security recipients. From way-back and specifically in 2011, the proposal which was very popular among the elite back then, was designed to cut the Social Security benefits of current and future retirees.

The "experts" figured out a way to change the formula used to calculate the cost-of-living adjustment (COLA) to stiff SS recipients. It is already bad. If Obama had his way, it would be worse. Just think, seniors actually believed that a man with these secret desires was actually going to give them a raise. It was never in Obama's plans.

Th notion called chained CPI, the Obama plan, was of course a betrayal to all Social Security beneficiaries according to a number of policy experts. It also would cut the benefits of people with disabilities and their families, children who have lost parents, and all other beneficiaries. It was simply a bad deal for seniors. Yet, Obama tried to convince everybody it was needed. Not so!

The Congressional Budget Office (CBO) estimated that the adoption of the so-called "Chained-CPI," which would be used to determine Social Security's annual COLA, would cut benefits by $112 billion over 10 years. It was seen as a great deal for the government that would save $112 Billion but no senior believed it should come out of the pockets of seniors who need Social Security benefits for everyday necessities.

The bottom line is that it would have cost seniors a lot of money but it would have been done sneakily so that nobody from the President's team could be blamed. The Social Security Administration Chief Actuary calculated the yearly loss in earnings for beneficiaries who retire at age 65 and receive average benefits at $560 less a year. With all the money Obama has as a multi-millionaire, I bet he is not out every year trying to give an extra $560.00 or $1000 to the government. At age 75, under the precepts of the law as written, SS recipients would get $1,000 less a year.

When the analysts suggest that the proposal will cut $1.6 trillion over Social Security's 75-year valuation period – mainly from the oldest of the old, primarily women and disproportionately poor, what seniors need to believe is that it was coming from their hide so that Obama could protect his hide.

Thankfully major senior citizen's advocacy groups lobbied to get Obama to change his mind. Obama was convinced that his election for a second term would be in jeopardy if he pushed the plan. Thankfully, it was never implemented. But, Obama did his best to keep raises in benefits from seniors. Yet, 40% of seniors if not more, still love the guy. Go figure.

Other books by Brian Kelly: (amazon.com, and Kindle)

Great Players in Alabama Football From Quarterbacks to offensive Linemen – the Greats!

Great Moments in Alabama Football AU Football from the start. This is the book.

Great Moments in Penn State Football PSU football from the start--games, coaches, players, etc.

Great Moments in Notre Dame Football ND Football from the start--games, coaches, players

Four Dollars & Sixty-Two Cents—A Christmas Story That Will Warm Your Heart!

My Red Hat Keeps Me on The Ground. Darraggh's Red Hat is really Magical

Seniors, Social Security & the Minimum Wage. Things seniors need to know.

How to Write Your First Book and Publish It with CreateSpace

The US Immigration Fix--It's all in here. Finally, an answer.

I had a Dream IBM Could be #1 Again _The title is self-explanatory

WineDiets.Com Presents The Wine Diet Learn how to lose weight while having fun.

Wilkes-Barre, PA; Return to Glory Wilkes-Barre City's return to glory

Geoffrey Parsons' Epoch... The Land of Fair Play Better than the original.

The Bill of Rights 4 Dummmies! This is the best book to learn about your rights.

Sol Bloom's Epoch ...Story of the Constitution The best book to learn the Constitution

America 4 Dummmies! All Americans should read to learn about this great country.

The Electoral College 4 Dummmies! How does it really work?

The All-Everything Machine Story about IBM's finest computer server.

Brian has written 98 books. Others can be found at amazon.com/author/brianwkelly

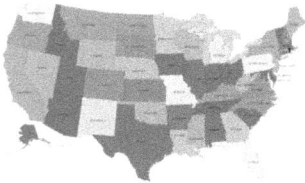